W9-DFT-062

THE YALE SHAKESPEARE

EDITED BY

WILBUR L. CROSS   TUCKER BROOKE

PUBLISHED UNDER THE DIRECTION
OF THE
DEPARTMENT OF ENGLISH, YALE UNIVERSITY,
ON THE FUND
GIVEN TO THE YALE UNIVERSITY PRESS IN 1917
BY THE MEMBERS OF THE
KINGSLEY TRUST ASSOCIATION
(SCROLL AND KEY SOCIETY OF YALE COLLEGE)
TO COMMEMORATE THE SEVENTY-FIFTH ANNIVERSARY
OF THE FOUNDING OF THE SOCIETY

THE TRAGEDY OF TROILUS AND CRESSIDA

EDITED BY

N. BURTON PARADISE

NEW HAVEN · YALE UNIVERSITY PRESS
LONDON · HUMPHREY MILFORD
OXFORD UNIVERSITY PRESS · MCMXXVII

CONTENTS

The facsimile opposite represents the title-page of the Elizabethan Club copy of the first issue of the only early quarto edition. Of this edition, four copies of the first issue and eleven of the second are known to survive. The Elizabethan Club copy contains the title-pages of both issues and the Epistle which was prefixed to the second.

THE
Historie of Troylus
and Cresseida.

As it was acted by the Kings Maiesties
seruants at the Globe.

Written by William Shakespeare.

LONDON
Imprinted by *G. Eld* for *R. Bonian* and *H. Walley*, and
are to be sold at the spred Eagle in Paules
Church-yeard, ouer against the
great North doore.
1609.

PRIAM, *King of Troy.*

HECTOR,
TROILUS,
PARIS, } *his Sons.*
DEIPHOBUS,
HELENUS,

MARGARELON, *a Bastard Son of Priam.*

ÆNEAS, } *Trojan Commanders.*
ANTENOR,

CALCHAS, *a Trojan Priest, taking part with the Greeks.*
PANDARUS, *Uncle to Cressida.*
AGAMEMNON, *the Greek General.*
MENELAUS, *his Brother.*

ACHILLES,
AJAX,
ULYSSES,
NESTOR, } *Greek Commanders.*
DIOMEDES,
PATROCLUS,

THERSITES, *a deformed and scurrilous Greek.*
ALEXANDER, *Servant to Cressida.*
Servant to Troilus.
Servant to Paris.
Servant to Diomedes.

HELEN, *Wife to Menelaus.*
ANDROMACHE, *Wife to Hector.*
CASSANDRA, *Daughter to Priam; a prophetess.*
CRESSIDA, *Daughter to Calchas.*

Trojan and Greek Soldiers, and Attendants.

SCENE: *Troy, and the Greek Camp before it.*]

The Dramatis Personæ were first supplied, imperfectly, by Rowe (ed. 1709), and later completed by Theobald (ed. 1733).

[*A Never Writer, to an Ever Reader. News.*

Eternal reader, you have here a new play, never stal'd with the Stage, never clapper-claw'd with the palms of the vulgar, and yet passing full of the palm comical, for it is a birth of your brain that 4 never undertook anything comical vainly. And were but the vain names of comedies changed for the titles of commodities, or of plays for pleas, you should see all those grand censors, that now 8 style them such vanities, flock to them for the main grace of their gravities, especially this author's comedies, that are so fram'd to the life that they serve for the most common commentaries of all 12 the actions of our lives, showing such a dexterity and power of wit that the most displeased with plays are pleas'd with his comedies. And all such dull and heavy-witted worldlings as were never 16 capable of the wit of a comedy, coming by report of them to his representations, have found that wit there that they never found in themselves and have parted better witted than they came, feel- 20 ing an edge of wit set upon them more than ever they dreamed they had brain to grind it on. So much and such savored salt of wit is in his come- dies that they seem, for their height of pleasure, 24 to be born in that sea that brought forth Venus. Amongst all there is none more witty than this: and had I time I would comment upon it, though I know it needs not, for so much as will make you 28 think your testern well bestowed, but for so much

[A Never Writer; *cf. n.*
29 testern: *sixpence (the price of the quarto)*

worth as even poor I know to be stuff'd in it. It
deserves such a labour as well as the best comedy
in Terence or Plautus. And believe this, that 32
when he is gone and his comedies out of sale, you
will scramble for them and set up a new English
Inquisition. Take this for a warning, and at the
peril of your pleasure's loss and judgment's, re- 36
fuse not nor like this the less for not being sullied
with the smoky breath of the multitude, but thank
fortune for the scape it hath made amongst you,
since by the grand possessors' wills I believe you 40
should have pray'd for them rather than been
pray'd. And so I leave all such to be pray'd for,
for the state of their wits' healths, that will not
praise it. Vale.]   44

THE PROLOGUE

[*Enter Chorus.*]

In Troy there lies the scene. From isles of Greece
The princes orgulous, their high blood chaf'd,
Have to the port of Athens sent their ships,
Fraught with the ministers and instruments   4
Of cruel war. Sixty and nine, that wore
Their crownets regal, from th' Athenian bay
Put forth toward Phrygia; and their vow is made
To ransack Troy, within whose strong immures   8
The ravish'd Helen, Menelaus' queen,
With wanton Paris sleeps; and that's the quarrel.
To Tenedos they come,
And the deep-drawing barks do there disgorge   12
Their warlike fraughtage. Now on Dardan plains
The fresh and yet unbruised Greeks do pitch
Their brave pavilions. Priam's six-gated city,
Dardan, and Tymbria, Ilias, Chetas, Troyan,   16
And Antenonidus, with massy staples
And corresponsive and fulfilling bolts,
Sperr up the sons of Troy.
Now expectation, tickling skittish spirits,   20
On one and other side, Troyan and Greek,
Sets all on hazard. And hither am I come,
A prologue arm'd, but not in confidence
Of author's pen or actor's voice, but suited   24
In like conditions as our argument,

The Prologue; *cf. n.*   2 orgulous: *proud*
4 Fraught: *laden*   6 crownets: *coronets*
8 ransack: *lay waste*   immures: *walls*
13 fraughtage: *cargoes*   Dardan: *Dardanian, Trojan*
15 brave: *splendid*   17 Antenonidus; *cf. n.*   massy: *huge*
18 corresponsive: *answering, fitting*   fulfilling: *complementary*
19 Sperr up: *shut up; cf. n.*   22 on hazard: *at stake*
23-25 A . . . argument; *cf. n.*   24 suited: *clothed*
25 argument: *story*

To tell you, fair beholders, that our play
Leaps o'er the vaunt and firstlings of those broils,
Beginning in the middle, starting thence away　　28
To what may be digested in a play.
Like or find fault; do as your pleasures are:
Now good or bad, 'tis but the chance of war.

[Exit.]

27　vaunt: *van, beginning*　　firstlings: *first-fruits*　　broils: *quarrels*
29　digested in: *reduced into*

The Tragedy of Troilus and Cressida

ACT FIRST

Scene One

[Troy. Before Priam's Palace]

Enter Pandarus and Troilus.

Tro. Call here my varlet, I'll unarm again.
Why should I war without the walls of Troy,
That find such cruel battle here within?
Each Troyan that is master of his heart,   4
Let him to field; Troilus, alas! hath none.

Pan. Will this gear ne'er be mended?

Tro. The Greeks are strong, and skilful to their strength,
Fierce to their skill, and to their fierceness valiant; 8
But I am weaker than a woman's tear,
Tamer than sleep, fonder than ignorance,
Less valiant than the virgin in the night,
And skilless as unpractis'd infancy.   12

Pan. Well, I have told you enough of this. For my part, I'll not meddle nor make no farther. He that will have a cake out of the wheat must needs tarry the grinding.   16

Tro. Have I not tarried?

Pan. Ay, the grinding; but you must tarry the bolting.

Tro. Have I not tarried?   20

Act First; *cf. n.*
1 varlet: *son of a gentleman acting as servant to a knight*
6 gear: *affair*   mended: *set right*   7 to: *in addition to*
10 fonder: *more foolish*   12 unpractis'd: *inexperienced*
14 make: *do*   19 bolting: *sifting, refining*

Pan. Ay, the bolting; but you must tarry the leavening.

Tro. Still have I tarried.

Pan. Ay, to the leavening; but here's yet in 24 the word 'hereafter' the kneading, the making of the cake, the heating of the oven, and the baking; nay, you must stay the cooling too, or you may chance to burn your lips.   28

Tro. Patience herself, what goddess e'er she be,
Doth lesser blench at sufferance than I do.
At Priam's royal table do I sit;
And when fair Cressid comes into my thoughts,— 32
So, traitor, then she comes, when she is thence.

Pan. Well, she looked yesternight fairer than ever I saw her look, or any woman else.

Tro. I was about to tell thee, when my heart, 36
As wedged with a sigh, would rive in twain,
Lest Hector or my father should perceive me:
I have—as when the sun doth light a storm—
Buried this sigh in wrinkle of a smile;   40
But sorrow, that is couch'd in seeming gladness,
Is like that mirth fate turns to sudden sadness.

Pan. An her hair were not somewhat darker than Helen's,—well, go to,—there were no more 44 comparison between the women: but, for my part, she is my kinswoman; I would not, as they term it, praise her, but I would somebody had heard her talk yesterday, as I did. I will not 48 dispraise your sister Cassandra's wit, but—

Tro. O Pandarus! I tell thee, Pandarus,—
When I do tell thee, there my hopes lie drown'd,

---

22 leavening: *fermenting (of dough)*   29 what: *what kind of*
30 blench: *flinch*   sufferance: *endurance*
33 So . . . thence; *cf. n.*   37 rive: *split*
39 a storm; *cf. n.*   41 couch'd: *lying concealed*
43 An: *if*   44 go to: *never mind*

Reply not in how many fathoms deep   52
They lie indrench'd. I tell thee I am mad
In Cressid's love; thou answer'st, she is fair;
Pour'st in the open ulcer of my heart
Her eyes, her hair, her cheek, her gait, her voice;   56
Handlest in thy discourse, O! that her hand,
In whose comparison all whites are ink,
Writing their own reproach; to whose soft seizure
The cygnet's down is harsh, and spirit of sense   60
Hard as the palm of ploughman. This thou tell'st me,
As true thou tell'st me, when I say I love her;
But, saying thus, instead of oil and balm,
Thou lay'st in every gash that love hath given me   64
The knife that made it.

> *Pan.* I speak no more than truth.

> *Tro.* Thou dost not speak so much.

> *Pan.* Faith, I'll not meddle in 't. Let her be 68
as she is. If she be fair, 'tis the better for her;
an she be not, she has the mends in her own
hands.

Tro. What! art thou angry, Pandarus? what! with
> me?

> *Pan.* Because she's kin to me, therefore she's
not so fair as Helen. An she were not kin to me,
she would be as fair on Friday as Helen is on 80
Sunday. But what care I? I care not an she

Tro. Good Pandarus! how now, Pandarus?   72

> *Pan.* I have had my labour for my travail;
ill-thought on of her, and ill-thought on of
you; gone between, and between, but small
thanks for my labour.   76

---

53 indrench'd: *immersed*
58 In whose comparison: *in comparison with which*
59 seizure: *grasp*
60 cygnet: *young swan*   spirit of sense; *cf. n.*
70 mends: *remedy*   73 travail: *toil*
80, 81 as fair . . . Sunday; *cf. n.*

were a blackamoor; 'tis all one to me.

Tro. Say I she is not fair?

   *   *Pan.* I do not care whether you do or no. 84
She's a fool to stay behind her father; let her
to the Greeks; and so I'll tell her the next time
I see her. For my part, I'll meddle nor make
no more i' th' matter.   88

Tro. Pandarus,—

   Pan. Not I.

Tro. Sweet Pandarus,—

   Pan. Pray you, speak no more to me! I will 92
leave all as I found it, and there an end.

                       Exit Pand[*arus*]. *Sound Alarum.*

Tro. Peace, you ungracious clamours! Peace, rude
   sounds!

Fools on both sides! Helen must needs be fair,
When with your blood you daily paint her thus.   96
I cannot fight upon this argument;
It is too starv'd a subject for my sword.
But Pandarus,—O gods, how do you plague me!
I cannot come to Cressid but by Pandar;   100
And he's as tetchy to be woo'd to woo
As she is stubborn-chaste against all suit.
Tell me, Apollo, for thy Daphne's love,
What Cressid is, what Pandar, and what we?   104
Her bed is India; there she lies, a pearl;
Between our Ilium and where she resides
Let it be call'd the wild and wand'ring flood,
Ourself the merchant, and this sailing Pandar   108
Our doubtful hope, our convoy and our bark.

         Alarum. Enter Æneas.

82 blackamoor: *Ethiopian*
94 ungracious: *unpleasing*
101 tetchy: *fretful, peevish*
109 convoy: *conveyance*

85 She's . . . father; *cf. n.*
97 I . . . argument; *cf. n.*
103 Daphne's; *cf. n.*

Æne. How now, Prince Troilus! wherefore not
  afield?

Tro. Because not there.   This woman's answer sorts,
For womanish it is to be from thence.   112
What news, Æneas, from the field to-day?

Æne. That Paris is returned home, and hurt.

Tro. By whom, Æneas?

Æne.   Troilus, by Menelaus.

Tro. Let Paris bleed; 'tis but a scar to scorn.   116
Paris is gor'd with Menelaus' horn.   *Alarum.*

Æne. Hark, what good sport is out of town to-day!

Tro. Better at home, if 'would I might' were 'may.'
But to the sport abroad.   Are you bound thither?   120

Æne. In all swift haste.

Tro.   Come, go we then together.
                                   Exeunt.

Scene Two

[*The Same.   A Street*]

Enter Cressid and [*Alexander*] *her man.*

Cres. Who were those went by?

Man.   Queen Hecuba and Helen.

Cres. And whither go they?

Man.   Up to the eastern tower,
Whose height commands as subject all the vale,
To see the battle.   Hector, whose patience   4
Is as a virtue fix'd, to-day was mov'd.
He chid Andromache, and struck his armourer,
And, like as there were husbandry in war,
Before the sun rose he was harness'd light,   8
And to the field goes he, where every flower

111 sorts: *fits*   116 scar: *wound*   117 Menelaus' horn; *cf. n.*
5 Is . . . fix'd; *cf. n.*
8 harness'd light: *clad in light armor*   7 husbandry: *thrift, diligence*

Did, as a prophet, weep what it foresaw
In Hector's wrath.

    Cres.   What was his cause of anger?

    Man. The noise goes, this: there is among the
Greeks   12
A lord of Troyan blood, nephew to Hector;
They call him Ajax.

    Cres.   Good; and what of him?

    Man. They say he is a very man *per se*
And stands alone.   16

    Cres. So do all men, unless they are drunk,
sick, or have no legs.

    Man. This man, lady, hath robb'd many
beasts of their particular additions: he is as 20
valiant as the lion, churlish as the bear, slow as
the elephant; a man into whom nature hath so
crowded humours that his valour is crush'd into
folly, his folly sauced with discretion. There is 24
no man hath a virtue that he hath not a glimpse
of, nor any man an attaint but he carries some
stain of it. He is melancholy without cause, and
merry against the hair. He hath the joints of 28
everything, but everything so out of joint that
he is a gouty Briareus, many hands and no use,
or purblinded Argus, all eyes and no sight.

    Cres. But how should this man, that makes 32
me smile, make Hector angry?

    Man. They say he yesterday cop'd Hector in
the battle and struck him down, the disdain

---

12 noise: *rumor*   13 nephew: *i.e. first cousin*
15 a . . . se: *preëminent in excellence*
20 particular additions: *peculiar characteristics*
21 churlish: *rough, violent*   23 humours: *caprices, whims; cf. n.*
23, 24 valour . . . discretion; *cf. n.*   25 glimpse of: *tinge of*
26 attaint: *fault, stain on honor*   27 stain: *tincture*
28 against the hair: *contrary to the natural tendency*
30 Briareus; *cf. n.*   31 Argus; *cf. n.*
34 cop'd: *met and fought with*   35 disdain: *vexation*

and shame whereof hath ever since kept Hector 36
fasting and waking.

Cres. Who comes here?

Enter Pandarus.

Man. Madam, your uncle Pandarus.

Cres. Hector's a gallant man. 40

Man. As may be in the world, lady.

Pan. What's that? What's that?

Cres. Good morrow, uncle Pandarus.

Pan. Good morrow, cousin Cressid. What 44
do you talk of? Good morrow, Alexander.
How do you, cousin? When were you at Ilium?

Cres. This morning, uncle.

Pan. What were you talking of when I 48
came? Was Hector armed and gone ere ye
came to Ilium? Helen was not up, was she?

Cres. Hector was gone, but Helen was not up.

Pan. E'en so; Hector was stirring early. 52

Cres. That were we talking of, and of his anger.

Pan. Was he angry?

Cres. So he says here.

Pan. True, he was so. I know the cause too. 56
He'll lay about him to-day, I can tell them that;
and there's Troilus will not come far behind
him. Let them take heed of Troilus, I can tell
them that too. 60

Cres. What! is he angry too?

Pan. Who, Troilus? Troilus is the better
man of the two.

Cres. O Jupiter! there's no comparison. 64

Pan. What! not between Troilus and Hector?
Do you know a man if you see him?

44 cousin: *niece; cf. n.*   46 Ilium; *cf. n.*

Cres. Ay, if I ever saw him before and knew
him.   68

Pan. Well, I say Troilus is Troilus.

Cres. Then you say as I say; for I am sure
he is not Hector.

Pan. No, nor Hector is not Troilus in some 72
degrees.

Cres. 'Tis just to each of them; he is himself.

Pan. Himself? Alas, poor Troilus, I would
he were.   76

Cres. So he is.

Pan. Condition, I had gone bare-foot to India.

Cres. He is not Hector.

Pan. Himself? no, he's not himself. Would 80
a' were himself! Well, the gods are above;
time must friend or end. Well, Troilus, well, I
would my heart were in her body. No, Hector
is not a better man than Troilus.   84

Cres. Excuse me.

Pan. He is elder.

Cres. Pardon me, pardon me.

Pan. Th' other's not come to 't; you shall tell 88
me another tale when th' other's come to 't.
Hector shall not have his will this year.

Cres. He shall not need it if he have his own.

Pan. Nor his qualities.   92

Cres. No matter.

Pan. Nor his beauty.

Cres. 'Twould not become him; his own's
better.   96

Pan. You have no judgment, niece. Helen
herself swore th' other day, that Troilus, for a

72, 73 in . . . degrees: *by many degrees*
78 Condition . . . India; *cf. n.*
82 friend or end: *kill or cure*   81 a': *he*
90 will; *cf. n.*   88 come to 't: *reached maturity*
                                     92 qualities: *natural gifts*

brown favour—for so 'tis, I must confess,—not
brown neither,—   100

Cres. No, but brown.

Pan. Faith, to say truth, brown and not
brown.

Cres. To say the truth, true and not true.   104

Pan. She prais'd his complexion above Paris.

Cres. Why, Paris hath colour enough.

Pan. So he has.

Cres. Then Troilus should have too much. If 108
she praised him above, his complexion is higher
than his. He having colour enough, and the
other higher, is too flaming a praise for a good
complexion. I had as lief Helen's golden tongue 112
had commended Troilus for a copper nose.

Pan. I swear to you, I think Helen loves him
better than Paris.

Cres. Then she's a merry Greek indeed.   116

Pan. Nay, I am sure she does. She came to
him th' other day into the compassed window,
and, you know, he has not past three or four
hairs on his chin,—   120

Cres. Indeed, a tapster's arithmetic may soon
bring his particulars therein to a total.

Pan. Why, he is very young; and yet will he,
within three pound, lift as much as his brother 124
Hector.

Cres. Is he so young a man, and so old a
lifter?

Pan. But to prove to you that Helen loves 128
him, she came and puts me her white hand to
his cloven chin,—

99 favour: *complexion, face*   116 merry Greek; *cf. n.*
118 compassed window: *semicircular bay window*
121 tapster's arithmetic: *small knowledge of figures*
127 lifter: *thief*

Cres. Juno have mercy! how came it cloven?

Pan. Why, you know, 'tis dimpled. I think 132
his smiling becomes him better than any man
in all Phrygia.

Cres. O! he smiles valiantly.

Pan. Does he not?   136

Cres. O, yes, an 'twere a cloud in autumn.

Pan. Why, go to, then. But to prove to you
that Helen loves Troilus,—

Cres. Troilus will stand to the proof, if 140
you'll prove it so.

Pan. Troilus! Why, he esteems her no more
than I esteem an addle egg.

Cres. If you love an addle egg as well as you 144
love an idle head, you would eat chickens i' th'
shell.

Pan. I cannot choose but laugh, to think
how she tickled his chin. Indeed, she has a 148
marvell's white hand, I must needs confess,—

Cres. Without the rack.

Pan. And she takes upon her to spy a white
hair on his chin.   152

Cres. Alas, poor chin! many a wart is richer.

Pan. But there was such laughing: Queen
Hecuba laughed that her eyes ran o'er.

Cres. With millstones.   156

Pan. And Cassandra laughed.

Cres. But there was more temperate fire under
the pot of her eyes. Did her eyes run o'er too?

Pan. And Hector laughed.   160

Cres. At what was all this laughing?

---

143 addle: *addled*   149 marvell's: *marvellous*
150 Without the rack: *i.e. without being tortured to force a confession*
156 With millstones; *cf. n.*

Pan. Marry, at the white hair that Helen spied on Troilus' chin.

Cres. An't had been a green hair, I should 164 have laughed too.

Pan. They laughed not so much at the hair as at his pretty answer.

Cres. What was his answer? 168

Pan. Quoth she, 'Here's but two-and-fifty hairs on your chin, and one of them is white.'

Cres. This is her question.

Pan. That's true; make no question of that. 172 'Two-and-fifty hairs,' quoth he, 'and one white. That white hair is my father, and all the rest are his sons.' 'Jupiter!' quoth she, 'which of these hairs is Paris, my husband?' 'The forked one,' 176 quoth he; 'pluck't out, and give it him.' But there was such laughing, and Helen so blushed, and Paris so chafed, and all the rest so laughed, that it passed. 180

Cres. So let it now, for it has been a great while going by.

Pan. Well, cousin, I told you a thing yesterday; think on 't. 184

Cres. So I do.

Pan. I'll be sworn 'tis true; he will weep you, an 'twere a man born in April.

Cres. And I'll spring up in his tears, an 188 'twere a nettle against May.　　　*Sound a retreat.*

Pan. Hark! they are coming from the field. Shall we stand up here, and see them as they pass toward Ilium? Good niece, do; sweet niece, Cressida. 192

Cres. At your pleasure.

162 Marry: *by (the Virgin) Mary*　　　167 pretty: *apt, witty*
169 two-and-fifty; *cf. n.*　　171 question: *subject (and also inquiry)*
180 passed: *went beyond all bounds*　　　187 an: *as if*
189 against: *just before*

Pan. Here, here, here's an excellent place; here we may see most bravely. I'll tell you them all by their names as they pass by, but mark 196 Troilus above the rest.

Cres. Speak not so loud.

Enter Æneas [passing across the stage].

Pan. That's Æneas. Is not that a brave man? He's one of the flowers of Troy, I can tell 200 you. But mark Troilus; you shall see anon.

Enter Antenor [passing across the stage].

Cres. Who's that?

Pan. That's Antenor. He has a shrewd wit, I can tell you; and he's a man good enough: 204 he's one o' the soundest judgment in Troy, whosoever, and a proper man of person. When comes Troilus? I'll show you Troilus anon. If he see me, you shall see him nod at me.   208

Cres. Will he give you the nod?

Pan. You shall see.

Cres. If he do, the rich shall have more.

Enter Hector [passing across the stage].

Pan. That's Hector, that, that, look you, that; 212 there's a fellow! Go thy way, Hector! There's a brave man, niece. O brave Hector! Look how he looks! There's a countenance! Is 't not a brave man?   216

Cres. O, a brave man!

Pan. Is a' not? It does a man's heart good. Look you what hacks are on his helmet! Look you yonder, do you see? Look you there; there's 220

195 bravely: *finely*   201 anon: *presently*
206 proper . . . person: *of handsome appearance*
211 rich . . . more; *cf.n.*   213 Go thy way: *peace be with you*

no jesting; there's laying on, take 't off who
will, as they say. There be hacks!

Cres. Be those with swords?

Pan. Swords? anything, he cares not; an 224
the devil come to him, it's all one. By God's lid,
it does one's heart good. Yonder comes Paris,
yonder comes Paris.

Enter Paris [passing across the stage].

Look ye yonder, niece. Is 't not a gallant man 228
too, is 't not? Why, this is brave now. Who
said he came hurt home to-day? He's not hurt.
Why, this will do Helen's heart good now, ha!
Would I could see Troilus now! You shall see 232
Troilus anon.

Cres. Who's that?

Enter Helenus [passing across the stage].

Pan. That's Helenus. I marvel where Troilus
is. That's Helenus. I think he went not forth 236
to-day. That's Helenus.

Cres. Can Helenus fight, uncle?

Pan. Helenus? No. Yes, he'll fight indifferent
well. I marvel where Troilus is. Hark! do you 240
not hear the people cry, 'Troilus?' Helenus is
a priest.

Cres. What sneaking fellow comes yonder?

Enter Troilus [passing across the stage].

Pan. Where? Yonder? That's Deiphobus. 244
'Tis Troilus! There's a man, niece! Hem! Brave
Troilus! the prince of chivalry!

Cres. Peace! for shame, peace!

Pan. Mark him; note him. O brave Troilus! 248

221 there's laying on; *cf. n.*   take 't off: *decry it*
225 God's lid: *God's eyelid (a petty oath)*

Look well upon him, niece. Look you how his
sword is bloodied, and his helm more hack'd
than Hector's; and how he looks, and how he
goes! O admirable youth! he ne'er saw three- 252
and-twenty. Go thy way, Troilus, go thy way!
Had I a sister were a grace, or a daughter a
goddess, he should take his choice. O admirable
man! Paris? Paris is dirt to him; and I 256
warrant, Helen, to change, would give money to
boot.

Cres. Here come more.

Enter common soldiers.

Pan. Asses, fools, dolts! chaff and bran, chaff 260
and bran! porridge after meat! I could live
and die i' th' eyes of Troilus. Ne'er look, ne'er
look; the eagles are gone; crows and daws,
crows and daws! I had rather be such a man as 264
Troilus than Agamemnon and all Greece.

Cres. There is among the Greeks Achilles, a
better man than Troilus.

Pan. Achilles! a drayman, a porter, a very 268
camel.

Cres. Well, well.

Pan. 'Well, well!' Why, have you any discretion? Have you any eyes? Do you know 272
what a man is? Is not birth, beauty, good
shape, discourse, manhood, learning, gentleness,
virtue, youth, liberality, and so forth, the spice
and salt that season a man?   276

Cres. Ay, a minced man; and then to be

254 were: *who was*   257, 258 to boot: *into the bargain*
262 i' th' eyes of Troilus; *cf. n.*
269 camel: *awkward, hulking fellow*   274 discourse: *eloquence*
277 minced: *affected (with a quibble on the literal meaning)*

baked with no date in the pie, for then the
man's date's out.

Pan. You are such another woman! One knows 280
not at what ward you lie.

Cres. Upon my back, to defend my belly;
upon my wit, to defend my wiles; upon my
secrecy, to defend mine honesty; my mask, to 284
defend my beauty; and you, to defend all these:
and at all these wards I lie, at a thousand
watches.

Pan. Say one of your watches.   288

Cres. Nay, I'll watch you for that; and that's
one of the chiefest of them too. If I cannot
ward what I would not have hit, I can watch you
for telling how I took the blow; unless it swell 292
past hiding, and then it's past watching.

Pan. You are such another!

Enter [*Troilus'*] *Boy.*

Boy. Sir, my lord would instantly speak with
you.   296

Pan. Where?

Boy. At your own house. [There he unarms him.]

Pan. Good boy, tell him I come.   [*Exit Boy.*]
I doubt he be hurt. Fare ye well, good niece.   300

Cres. Adieu, uncle.

Pan. I'll be with you, niece, by and by.

Cres. To bring, uncle?

Pan. Ay, a token from Troilus.   304

Cres. By the same token, you are a bawd.

Exit Pand[*arus*].

---

278 date; *cf. n.*   280 You . . . woman: *what a woman you are*
281 at . . . lie; *cf. n.*   284 honesty: *honor*
287 watches; *cf. n.*
291, 292 watch . . . telling: *prevent you from telling*
300 doubt: *fear*   303 To bring; *cf. n.*

Words, vows, gifts, tears, and love's full sacrifice
He offers in another's enterprise;
But more in Troilus thousandfold I see   308
Than in the glass of Pandar's praise may be.
Yet hold I off.   Women are angels, wooing.
Things won are done, joy's soul lies in the doing.
That she belov'd knows nought that knows not this: 312
Men prize the thing ungain'd more than it is.
That she was never yet, that ever knew
Love got so sweet as when desire did sue.
Therefore this maxim out of love I teach: 316
Achievement is command; ungain'd, beseech.
That though my heart's contents firm love doth bear,
Nothing of that shall from mine eyes appear.   *Exit.*

Scene Three

[*The Greek Camp.   Before Agamemnon's Tent*]

*Sennet.   Enter Agamemnon, Nestor, Ulysses,
Diomedes, Menelaus, with others.*

Agam. Princes,
What grief hath set the jaundice on your cheeks?
The ample proposition that hope makes
In all designs begun on earth below   4
Fails in the promis'd largeness.   Checks and disasters
Grow in the veins of actions highest rear'd,
As knots, by the conflux of meeting sap,
Infect the sound pine and diverts his grain   8

---

310 wooing: *i.e. while being wooed*   312 she: *woman*
313 more . . . is: *above its real value*
317 Achievement . . . beseech: *cf. n.*
Scene Three S. d. Sennet: *set of notes played on a trumpet*
3 proposition: *promise*   5 Fails in: *fails to achieve*
7 conflux: *flowing together*   8 diverts: *i.e. divert; cf. n.*

Tortive and errant from his course of growth.
Nor, princes, is it matter new to us
That we come short of our suppose so far
That after seven years' siege yet Troy walls stand;   12
Sith every action that hath gone before,
Whereof we have record, trial did draw
Bias and thwart, not answering the aim
And that unbodied figure of the thought   16
That gave 't surmised shape.   Why then, you princes,
Do you with cheeks abash'd behold our works,
And think them shame? which are indeed nought else
But the protractive trials of great Jove,   20
To find persistive constancy in men;
The fineness of which metal is not found
In Fortune's love; for then, the bold and coward,
The wise and fool, the artist and unread,   24
The hard and soft, seem all affin'd and kin.
But, in the wind and tempest of her frown,
Distinction, with a loud and powerful fan,
Puffing at all, winnows the light away;   28
And what hath mass or matter, by itself
Lies rich in virtue and unmingled.

   Nest. With due observance of thy godlike seat,
Great Agamemnon, Nestor shall apply   32
Thy latest words.   In the reproof of chance
Lies the true proof of men. The sea being smooth,
How many shallow bauble boats dare sail
Upon her patient breast, making their way   36

9 Tortive: *distorted*   errant: *wandering*
11 suppose: *expectation*   13 Sith: *since*
13-17 *Cf. n.*   20 protractive: *long drawn out*
21 persistive: *persistent*
23 In Fortune's love: *when fortune smiles*
24 artist: *educated person*   25 affin'd: *related by affinity*
29 by itself: *alone, separate*
30 *Shows in the richness of unalloyed purity*
32 apply: *moralise on*   33 reproof: *scorning, rebuking*
35 bauble: *toy*

With those of nobler bulk!
But let the ruffian Boreas once enrage
The gentle Thetis, and anon behold
The strong-ribb'd bark through liquid mountains
    cut,   40
Bounding between the two moist elements,
Like Perseus' horse. Where's then the saucy boat,
Whose weak untimber'd sides but even now
Co-rivall'd greatness? Either to harbour fled,   44
Or made a toast for Neptune. Even so
Doth valour's show and valour's worth divide
In storms of fortune. For in her ray and brightness
The herd hath more annoyance by the breese   48
Than by the tiger; but when the splitting wind
Makes flexible the knees of knotted oaks,
And flies fled under shade, why then the thing of
    courage,
As rous'd with rage, with rage doth sympathize,   52
And with an accent tun'd in self-same key,
Retorts to chiding fortune.
   Ulyss.   Agamemnon,
Thou great commander, nerve and bone of Greece,
Heart of our numbers, soul and only spirit,   56
In whom the tempers and the minds of all
Should be shut up, hear what Ulysses speaks.
Besides the applause and approbation
The which, [*To Agamemnon*] most mighty for thy
    place and sway,   60
[*To Nestor*] And thou most reverend for thy stretch'd-
    out life,

38 Boreas: *the north wind*   39 Thetis: *the sea; cf. n.*
41 moist elements; *cf. n.*   42 Perseus' horse: *Pegasus; cf. n.*
45 toast: *a rich morsel to be swallowed (usually in a cup of wine)*
46 show: *external appearance*   48 breese: *gadfly*
51 fled: *are fled*   54 Retorts; *cf. n.*   55 nerve: *sinew*
57 tempers: *temperaments*   60 sway: *sovereignty*

I give to both your speeches, which were such
As Agamemnon and the hand of Greece
Should hold up high in brass; and such again   64
As venerable Nestor, hatch'd in silver,
Should with a bond of air, strong as the axle-tree
On which the heavens ride, knit all Greeks' ears
To his experienc'd tongue: yet let it please both,   68
Thou great, and wise, to hear Ulysses speak.

    Agam. Speak, Prince of Ithaca; and be 't of less
      expect
That matter needless, of importless burthen,
Divide thy lips, than we are confident,   72
When rank Thersites opes his mastic jaws,
We shall hear music, wit, and oracle.

    Ulyss. Troy, yet upon his basis, had been down,
And the great Hector's sword had lack'd a master,   76
But for these instances.
The specialty of rule hath been neglected;
And look, how many Grecian tents do stand
Hollow upon this plain, so many hollow factions.   80
When that the general is not like the hive
To whom the foragers shall all repair,
What honey is expected?   Degree being vizarded,
Th' unworthiest shows as fairly in the mask.   84
The heavens themselves, the planets, and this centre
Observe degree, priority, and place,
Insisture, course, proportion, season, form,
Office, and custom, in all line of order;   88

62-68 *Cf. n.*   67 knit: *join*
70 of less expect: *less to be expected*
71 importless: *insignificant*   burthen: *meaning*
73 rank: *rebellious or gross*   opes: *opens*   mastic; *cf. n.*
75-137 *Cf. n.*   75 his: *its*   basis: *foundation*
77 instances: *reasons*
78 specialty of rule: *particular rights of supreme authority*
83 Degree: *rank*   vizarded: *masked*   84 mask: *masquerade*
85 centre: *earth*   87 Insisture: *regularity*
88 Office: *function*   in . . . order: *all in order*

And therefore is the glorious planet Sol
In noble eminence enthron'd and spher'd
Amidst the other; whose med'cinable eye
Corrects the ill aspects of planets evil,   92
And posts, like the commandment of a king,
Sans check, to good and bad.   But when the planets
In evil mixture to disorder wander,
What plagues, and what portents, what mutiny,   96
What raging of the sea, shaking of earth,
Commotion in the winds, frights, changes, horrors,
Divert and crack, rend and deracinate
The unity and married calm of states   100
Quite from their fixure! O! when degree is shak'd,
Which is the ladder to all high designs,
The enterprise is sick.   How could communities,
Degrees in schools, and brotherhoods in cities,   104
Peaceful commerce from dividable shores,
The primogenitive and due of birth,
Prerogative of age, crowns, sceptres, laurels,
But by degree, stand in authentic place?   108
Take but degree away, untune that string,
And, hark! what discord follows! Each thing meets
In mere oppugnancy.   The bounded waters
Should lift their bosoms higher than the shores,   112
And make a sop of all this solid globe;
Strength should be lord of imbecility,
And the rude son should strike his father dead;
Force should be right; or rather, right and wrong, 116

89 Sol: *the sun*   91 other: *others*   med'cinable: *healing*
92 aspects; *cf. n.*   93 posts: *speeds*
94 Sans: *without*   96 mutiny: *discord*
99 deracinate: *uproot*   101 fixure: *fixed position, stability*
102 *By which men achieve all high purposes*
105 dividable: *separated*
106 primogenitive: *right of succession belonging to the eldest son*
108 authentic: *one's own, peculiar*
111 mere; *absolute*   oppugnancy: *conflict*
113 sop; *cf. n.*   114 imbecility: *weakness*

Between whose endless jar justice resides,
Should lose their names, and so should justice too.
Then everything includes itself in power,
Power into will, will into appetite;   120
And appetite, an universal wolf,
So doubly seconded with will and power,
Must make perforce an universal prey,
And last eat up himself. Great Agamemnon,   124
This chaos, when degree is suffocate,
Follows the choking.
And this neglection of degree is it
That by a pace goes backward, in a purpose   128
It hath to climb.   The general's disdain'd
By him one step below, he by the next,
That next by him beneath; so every step,
Exampled by the first pace that is sick   132
Of his superior, grows to an envious fever
Of pale and bloodless emulation:
And 'tis this fever that keeps Troy on foot,
Not her own sinews. To end a tale of length,   136
Troy in our weakness lives, not in her strength.

Nest. Most wisely hath Ulysses here discover'd
The fever whereof all our power is sick.

Agam. The nature of the sickness found, Ulysses, 140
What is the remedy?

Ulyss. The great Achilles, whom opinion crowns
The sinew and the forehand of our host,
Having his ear full of his airy fame,   144
Grows dainty of his worth, and in his tent
Lies mocking our designs. With him Patroclus
Upon a lazy bed the livelong day

117 jar: *discord*   119, 120 *Cf. n.*
125 suffocate: *suffocated*   127-129 And . . . climb; *cf. n.*
127 neglection: *neglect*   128 by a pace: *step by step*
132 Exampled: *furnished with a precedent*   sick: *envious*
138 discover'd: *exposed to view*   139 power: *army*
143 forehand: *mainstay; cf. n.*   145 Grows . . . worth; *cf. n.*

Breaks scurril jests,   148
And with ridiculous and awkward action—
Which, slanderer, he imitation calls—
He pageants us.   Sometime, great Agamemnon,
Thy topless deputation he puts on   152
And, like a strutting player, whose conceit
Lies in his hamstring, and doth think it rich
To hear the wooden dialogue and sound
'Twixt his stretch'd footing and the scaffoldage,— 156
Such to-be-pitied and o'er-wrested seeming
He acts thy greatness in; and when he speaks,
'Tis like a chime a-mending; with terms unsquar'd,
Which,   from   the   tongue   of   roaring   Typhon
        dropp'd,   160
Would seem hyperboles.   At this fusty stuff
The large Achilles, on his press'd bed lolling,
From his deep chest laughs out a loud applause;
Cries, 'Excellent! 'tis Agamemnon just.   164
Now play me Nestor; hem, and stroke thy beard,
As he being drest to some oration.'
That's done, as near as the extremest ends
Of parallels, as like as Vulcan and his wife,   168
Yet god Achilles still cries, 'Excellent!
'Tis Nestor right.   Now play him me, Patroclus,
Arming to answer in a night alarm.'
And then, forsooth, the faint defects of age   172
Must be the scene of mirth; to cough and spit,
And with a palsy fumbling on his gorget,

148 scurril: *scurrilous*   151 pageants: *mimics*
152 topless deputation: *supreme power deputed to a leader*
153 conceit: *mental faculty, understanding*
154 hamstring: *sinews of the legs*
156 stretch'd: *affected, exaggerated*   footing: *tread*   scaffoldage:
        stage
157 o'er-wrested: *strained; cf. n.*   seeming: *appearance, show*
159 unsquar'd: *unsuitable*   160 Typhon; *cf. n.*   161 fusty: *stale*
166 drest to: *prepared for*   167, 168 as . . . wife; *cf. n.*
170 right: *exactly*   171 answer: *present himself for service*
172 faint: *feeble*   174 gorget: *armor for the throat*

Shake in and out the rivet; and at this sport
Sir Valour dies; cries, 'O! enough, Patroclus;   176
Or give me ribs of steel; I shall split all
In pleasure of my spleen.' And in this fashion,
All our abilities, gifts, natures, shapes,
Severals and generals of grace exact,   180
Achievements, plots, orders, preventions,
Excitements to the field, or speech for truce,
Success or loss, what is or is not, serves
As stuff for these two to make paradoxes.   184
    Nest. And in the imitation of these twain—
Who, as Ulysses says, opinion crowns
With an imperial voice—many are infect.
Ajax is grown self-will'd, and bears his head   188
In such a rein, in full as proud a place
As broad Achilles; and keeps his tent like him;
Makes factious feasts; rails on our state of war,
Bold as an oracle, and sets Thersites—   192
A slave whose gall coins slanders like a mint—
To match us in comparisons with dirt;
To weaken and discredit our exposure,
How rank soever rounded in with danger.   196
    Ulyss. They tax our policy, and call it cowardice,
Count wisdom as no member of the war,
Forestall prescience, and esteem no act
But that of hand. The still and mental parts,   200
That do contrive how many hands shall strike,

176 Sir Valour: *i.e. Achilles*   dies: *i.e. from laughing*
178 spleen: *amusement*   180 *Cf. n.*
181 preventions: *precautionary measures*
182 Excitements: *incitements*   184 paradoxes: *absurdities*
186, 187 opinion . . . voice: *have great reputations*
187 infect: *infected*   188, 189 bears . . . rein: *is as haughty*
190 keeps: *remains in*
193 like a mint: *i.e. as fast as a mint coins money*
195 exposure: *i.e. to danger*
196 rank: *rankly, excessively*   rounded in: *hemmed in*
197 tax: *censure*   policy: *strategy*
198 no member of: *having no part in*
199 Forestall: *condemn beforehand*
200 still: *silent*

When fitness call them on, and know by measure
Of their observant toil the enemies' weight,—
Why, this hath not a finger's dignity.   204
They call this bed-work, mapp'ry, closet-war;
So that the ram that batters down the wall,
For the great swing and rudeness of his poise,
They place before his hand that made the engine, 208
Or those that with the fineness of their souls
By reason guide his execution.

   Nest. Let this be granted, and Achilles' horse
Makes many Thetis' sons.   *Tucket.* 212

   Agam. What trumpet? Look, Menelaus.

   Men. From Troy.

Enter Æneas.

   Agam. What would you 'fore our tent?

   Æne. Is this great Agamemnon's tent, I pray
   you?   216

   Agam. Even this.

   Æne. May one, that is a herald and a prince,
Do a fair message to his kingly ears?

   Agam. With surety stronger than Achilles' arm 220
'Fore all the Greekish heads, which with one voice
Call Agamemnon head and general.

   Æne. Fair leave and large security. How may
A stranger to those most imperial looks   224
Know them from eyes of other mortals?

   Agam.   How?

   Æne. Ay.
I ask, that I might waken reverence,
And on the cheek be ready with a blush   228
Modest as morning when she coldly eyes

---

202 fitness: *a proper time*   202, 203 know . . . weight; *cf. n.*
205 bed-work: *easy work, such as might be done in bed*   mapp'ry:
   map-making   212 *Cf. n.*   S. d. Tucket: *a trumpet call*
221 heads: *chiefs*   228 on; *cf. n.*

The youthful Phœbus.
Which is that god in office, guiding men?
Which is the high and mighty Agamemnon?   232

  Agam. This Troyan scorns us; or the men of Troy
Are ceremonious courtiers.

  Æne. Courtiers as free, as debonair, unarm'd,
As bending angels; that's their fame in peace;   236
But when they would seem soldiers, they have galls,
Good arms, strong joints, true swords; and, Jove's accord,
Nothing so full of heart. But peace, Æneas!
Peace, Troyan; lay thy finger on thy lips!   240
The worthiness of praise distains his worth,
If that the prais'd himself bring the praise forth;
But what the repining enemy commends,
That breath fame blows; that praise, sole pure, transcends.   244

  Agam. Sir, you of Troy, call you yourself Æneas?

  Æne. Ay, Greek, that is my name.

  Agam. What's your affair, I pray you?

  Æne. Sir, pardon; 'tis for Agamemnon's ears.   248

  Agam. He hears nought privately that comes from Troy.

  Æne. Nor I from Troy come not to whisper him:
I bring a trumpet to awake his ear,
To set his sense on the attentive bent,   252
And then to speak.

  Agam.   Speak frankly as the wind;
It is not Agamemnon's sleeping hour.
That thou shalt know, Troyan, he is awake,
He tells thee so himself.

237 galls: *strong passions*   238, 239 Jove's . . . heart; *cf. n.*
241 distains: *sullies*
244 sole pure: *alone, unalloyed by selfish motives*
252 To . . . bent: *to rouse his senses to attention*

Æne.   Trumpet, blow loud,   256
Send thy brass voice through all these lazy tents;
And every Greek of mettle, let him know,
What Troy means fairly shall be spoke aloud.
                              The Trumpets sound.
We have, great Agamemnon, here in Troy,   260
A prince called Hector,—Priam is his father,—
Who in this dull and long-continu'd truce
Is rusty grown.   He bade me take a trumpet,
And to this purpose speak.   Kings, princes, lords! 264
If there be one among the fair'st of Greece
That holds his honour higher than his ease,
That seeks his praise more than he fears his peril,
That knows his valour, and knows not his fear,   268
That loves his mistress more than in confession
With truant vows to her own lips he loves,
And dare avow her beauty and her worth
In other arms than hers,—to him this challenge.   272
Hector, in view of Troyans and of Greeks,
Shall make it good, or do his best to do it,
He hath a lady wiser, fairer, truer,
Than ever Greek did compass in his arms;   276
And will to-morrow with his trumpet call,
Mid-way between your tents and walls of Troy,
To rouse a Grecian that is true in love.
If any come, Hector shall honour him;   280
If none, he'll say in Troy when he retires,
The Grecian dames are sunburnt, and not worth
The splinter of a lance.   Even so much.
     Agam.   This shall be told our lovers, Lord
          Æneas;   284
If none of them have soul in such a kind,

---

270 truant: *unfaithful*   282 sunburnt: *i.e. not fair*
285 soul . . . kind: *spirit ready to take up the challenge*

We left them all at home.   But we are soldiers;
And may that soldier a mere recreant prove,
That means not, hath not, or is not in love!   288
If then one is, or hath, or means to be,
That one meets Hector; if none else, I'll be he.

  Nest. Tell him of Nestor, one that was a man
When Hector's grandsire suck'd.   He is old now, 292
But if there be not in our Grecian host
One nobleman that hath one spark of fire
To answer for his love, tell him from me,
I'll hide my silver beard in a gold beaver,   296
And in my vantbrace put this wither'd brawn,
And, meeting him, will tell him that my lady
Was fairer than his grandam, and as chaste
As may be in the world.   His youth in flood,   300
I'll prove this truth with my three drops of blood.

  Æne. Now heavens forbid such scarcity of youth!
  Ulyss. Amen.

  Agam. Fair Lord Æneas, let me touch your hand; 304
To our pavilion shall I lead you first.
Achilles shall have word of this intent;
So shall each lord of Greece, from tent to tent.
Yourself shall feast with us before you go,   308
And find the welcome of a noble foe.

                    Exeunt. Mane[n]t Ulysses and Nestor.
  Ulyss. Nestor!
  Nest. What says Ulysses?
  Ulyss. I have a young conception in my brain;   312
Be you my time to bring it to some shape.

293 host; *cf. n.*
296 beaver: *the part of a helmet which covered the face*
297 vantbrace: *armor for the forearm*
300 His . . . flood: *although he is at the high-tide of youth*
301 prove; *cf. n.*   306 intent: *intention*
309 S. d. Manent: *remain on the stage*
312 young conception: *new plan*   313 *Cf. n.*

Nest. What is 't?

Ulyss. This 'tis:

Blunt wedges rive hard knots; the seeded pride   316
That hath to this maturity blown up
In rank Achilles, must or now be cropp'd,
Or, shedding, breed a nursery of like evil,
To overbulk us all.

    Nest.   Well, and how?   320

    Ulyss. This challenge that the gallant Hector sends,
However it is spread in general name,
Relates in purpose only to Achilles.

    Nest. The purpose is perspicuous even as sub-
       stance   324
Whose grossness little characters sum up;
And, in the publication, make no strain,
But that Achilles, were his brain as barren
As banks of Libya,—though, Apollo knows,   328
'Tis dry enough,—will with great speed of judgment,
Ay, with celerity, find Hector's purpose
Pointing on him.

    Ulyss. And wake him to the answer, think you?   332

    Nest. Yes, 'tis most meet. Who may you else op-
       pose,
That can from Hector bring his honour off,
If not Achilles? Though 't be a sportful combat,
Yet in this trial much opinion dwells;   336
For here the Troyans taste our dear'st repute
With their fin'st palate; and trust to me, Ulysses,

316-319 seeded . . . evil; *cf. n.*   318 or: *either*
324 perspicuous: *apparent*   substance: *substantial wealth*
325 grossness: *bulkiness*   characters: *figures*
326 in the publication: *i.e. when Hector's challenge is proclaimed*
    make no strain: *do not doubt, be assured*
328 Libya: *the African desert*   329 dry: *stupid*
331 on: *at*   333 meet: *fitting*
335 sportful: *not in deadly earnest*
336 opinion: *credit, reputation*
                    337 dear'st: *most precious*

Our imputation shall be oddly pois'd
In this wild action; for the success,   340
Although particular, shall give a scantling
Of good or bad unto the general;
And in such indexes, although small pricks
To their subsequent volumes, there is seen   344
The baby figure of the giant mass
Of things to come at large.   It is suppos'd
He that meets Hector issues from our choice;
And choice, being mutual act of all our souls,   348
Makes merit her election, and doth boil,
As 'twere from forth us all, a man distill'd
Out of our virtues; who miscarrying,
What heart from hence receives the conqu'ring part, 352
To steel a strong opinion to themselves?
Which entertain'd, limbs are his instruments,
In no less working than are swords and bows
Directive by the limbs.   356
   Ulyss. Give pardon to my speech:
Therefore 'tis meet Achilles meet not Hector.
Let us, like merchants, show our foulest wares,
And think perchance they'll sell; if not,   360
The lustre of the better yet to show
Shall show the better.   Do not consent
That ever Hector and Achilles meet;
For both our honour and our shame in this   364
Are dogg'd with two strange followers.
   Nest. I see them not with my old eyes.   What are
     they?
   Ulyss. What glory our Achilles shares from Hector,
Were he not proud, we all should wear with him.   368
But he already is too insolent;

339-346 Our . . . large; *cf. n.*
339 imputation: *reputation*   oddly pois'd: *unequally balanced, i.e.*
    exposed to extraordinary risks   349 election: *basis of choice*
351-356 who . . . limbs; *cf. n.*   359 foulest: *most unattractive*

And we were better parch in Afric sun
Than in the pride and salt scorn of his eyes,
Should he 'scape Hector fair. If he were foil'd,   372
Why then we did our main opinion crush
In taint of our best man.   No; make a lottery;
And by device let blockish Ajax draw
The sort to fight with Hector; among ourselves   376
Give him allowance as the worthier man,
For that will physic the great Myrmidon
Who broils in loud applause; and make him fall
His crest that prouder than blue Iris bends.   380
If the dull brainless Ajax come safe off,
We'll dress him up in voices; if he fail,
Yet go we under our opinion still
That we have better men.   But, hit or miss,   384
Our project's life this shape of sense assumes:
Ajax employ'd plucks down Achilles' plumes.

   Nest. Now, Ulysses, I begin to relish thy advice;
And I will give a taste of it forthwith   388
To Agamemnon.   Go we to him straight.
Two curs shall tame each other; pride alone
Must tarre the mastiffs on, as 'twere their bone.

                            Exeunt.

371 salt: *bitter*   372 foil'd: *defeated*
373 main opinion: *general reputation*   374 taint: *disgrace*
375 device: *stratagem*   blockish: *stupid*   376 sort: *lot*
377 allowance: *recognition*   378 Myrmidon; *cf. n.*
379 broils in: *is feverish with*   fall: *lower*
380 Iris: *the rainbow*
382 dress . . . voices: *deck him in praises*
                                        391 tarre: *incite*

ACT SECOND

Scene One

[A Part of the Greek Camp]

Enter Ajax and Thersites.

Ajax. Thersites!

Ther. Agamemnon, how if he had boils? full, all over, generally?

Ajax. Thersites!   4

Ther. And those boils did run? Say so, did not the general run [then]? Were not that a botchy core?

Ajax. Dog!   8

Ther. Then would come some matter from him. I see none now.

Ajax. Thou bitch-wolf's son, canst thou not hear? Feel then.   *Strikes him.* 12

Ther. The plague of Greece upon thee, thou mongrel beef-witted lord!

Ajax. Speak then, you vinewed'st leaven, speak. I will beat thee into handsomeness.   16

Ther. I shall sooner rail thee into wit and holiness; but I think thy horse will sooner con an oration than thou learn a prayer without book. Thou canst strike, canst thou? A red 20 murrain o' thy jade's tricks!

Ajax. Toadstool, learn me the proclamation.

Ther. Dost thou think I have no sense, thou strik'st me thus?   24

7 botchy: *broken-out*   9 matter; *cf. n.*
14 mongrel; *cf. n.*   beef-witted: *thick-headed*
15 vinewed'st: *most mouldy; cf. n.*   16 handsomeness: *civility*
18 con: *learn*   19, 20 without book: *by heart*
21 murrain: *plague*   jade's tricks: *i.e. tricks of a vicious horse*
22 learn me: *find out for me*   23 sense: *feeling*

Ajax. The proclamation!

Ther. Thou art proclaim'd a fool, I think.

Ajax. Do not, porpentine, do not; my fingers itch.   28

Ther. I would thou didst itch from head to foot, and I had the scratching of thee; I would make thee the loathsom'st scab in Greece. [When thou art forth in the incursions, thou 32 strikest as slow as another.]

Ajax. I say, the proclamation!

Ther. Thou grumblest and railest every hour on Achilles, and thou art as full of envy at his 36 greatness as Cerberus is at Proserpina's beauty, ay that thou bark'st at him.

Ajax. Mistress Thersites!

Ther. Thou shouldst strike him.   40

Ajax. Cobloaf!

Ther. He would pun thee into shivers with his fist, as a sailor breaks a biscuit.

Ajax. You whoreson cur.   [*Beating him.*] 44

Ther. Do, do.

Ajax. Thou stool for a witch!

Ther. Ay, do, do; thou sodden-witted lord! thou hast no more brain than I have in mine 48 elbows; an asinego may tutor thee. Thou scurvy-valiant ass, thou art here but to thrash Troyans; and thou art bought and sold among those of any wit, like a barbarian slave. If thou use to 52 beat me, I will begin at thy heel, and tell what thou art by inches, thou thing of no bowels, thou!

27 porpentine: *porcupine*   32 incursions: *raids*
37 Cerberus; *cf. n.*   41 Cobloaf: *a little loaf with a round head*
42 pun: *pound*   shivers: *splinters*
44 whoreson: *bastard, scurvy*   46 stool . . . witch; *cf. n.*
49 asinego: *little ass*
51 bought and sold: *made a fool of (a proverbial expression)*
52 use: *make a practice*   54 bowels: *compassion*

    Ajax. You dog!

    Ther. You scurvy lord!   56

    Ajax. You cur!   *[Beating him.]*

    Ther. Mars his idiot! do, rudeness; do, camel; do, do.

        Enter Achilles and Patroclus.

    Achil. Why, how now, Ajax! wherefore do you
    this?   60

How now, Thersites! what's the matter, man?

    Ther. You see him there, do you?

    Achil. Ay; what's the matter?

    Ther. Nay, look upon him.   64

    Achil. So I do. What's the matter?

    Ther. Nay, but regard him well.

    Achil. 'Well!' why, I do so.

    Ther. But yet you look not well upon him; 68
for, whosomever you take him to be, he is Ajax.

    Achil. I know that, fool.

    Ther. Ay, but that fool knows not himself.

    Ajax. Therefore I beat thee.   72

    Ther. Lo, lo, lo, lo, what modicums of wit he
utters! His evasions have ears thus long. I have
bobb'd his brain more than he has beat my
bones. I will buy nine sparrows for a penny, and 76
his *pia mater* is not worth the ninth part of a
sparrow. This lord, Achilles, Ajax, who wears
his wit in his belly, and his guts in his head, I'll
tell you what I say of him.   80

    Achil. What?

    Ther. I say, this Ajax,—

             [Ajax offers to strike him.]

    Achil. Nay, good Ajax.

---

74 evasions . . . long: *his quibbles are those of an ass*
75 bobb'd: *thumped, buffeted*   77 pia mater: *brain*

Ther. Has not so much wit—   84
[*Ajax again offers to strike him.*]

Achil. Nay, I must hold you.

Ther. As will stop the eye of Helen's needle,
for whom he comes to fight.

Achil. Peace, fool!   88

Ther. I would have peace and quietness, but
the fool will not—he there, that he. Look you
there.

Ajax. O thou damned cur! I shall—   92

Achil. Will you set your wit to a fool's?

Ther. No, I warrant you; for a fool's will
shame it.

Patr. Good words, Thersites.   96

Achil. What's the quarrel?

Ajax. I bade the vile owl go learn me the
tenour of the proclamation, and he rails upon
me.   100

Ther. I serve thee not.

Ajax. Well, go to, go to.

Ther. I serve here voluntary.

Achil. Your last service was sufferance, 'twas 104
not voluntary; no man is beaten voluntary.
Ajax was here the voluntary, and you as under
an impress.

Ther. E'en so. A great deal of your wit, too, 108
lies in your sinews, or else there be liars. Hector
shall have a great catch if he knock out either of
your brains. He were as good crack a fusty nut
with no kernel.   112

Achil. What, with me too, Thersites?

Ther. There's Ulysses and old Nestor, whose

93 set: *oppose*   103 voluntary: *as a volunteer*
104 sufferance: *suffering (with a quibble on the meaning 'by permis-*
sion')
107 impress: *enforced levy*   111 were as good: *had as well*

wit was mouldy ere your grandsires had nails
on their toes, yoke you like draught-oxen, and 116
make you plough up the war.

Achil. What, what?

Ther. Yes, good sooth. To Achilles, to Ajax,
to—   120

Ajax. I shall cut out your tongue.

Ther. 'Tis no matter; I shall speak as much
as thou afterwards.

Patr. No more words, Thersites; peace!   124

Ther. I will hold my peace when Achilles'
brach bids me, shall I?

Achil. There's for you, Patroclus.

Ther. I will see you hanged, like clotpoles, 128
ere I come any more to your tents. I will keep
where there is wit stirring and leave the faction
of fools.   *Exit.*

Patr. A good riddance.   132

Achil. Marry, this, sir, is proclaim'd through all our
   host:

That Hector, by the fifth hour of the sun,
Will, with a trumpet, 'twixt our tents and Troy
To-morrow morning call some knight to arms   136
That hath a stomach; and such a one that dare
Maintain—I know not what; 'tis trash.   Farewell.

Ajax. Farewell.   Who shall answer him?

Achil. I know not.   'Tis put to lottery.   Otherwise,   140
He knew his man.

Ajax. O, meaning you.   I will go learn more of it.
                         Exeunt.

115 your; *cf. n.*   119 good sooth: *truly, indeed*
119, 120 To . . . to; *cf. n.*   126 brach: *bitch-hound; cf. n.*
128 clotpoles: *blockheads*   137 stomach: *appetite for fighting*

Scene Two

[Troy.   A Room in Priam's Palace]

Enter Priam, Hector, Troilus, Paris, and Helenus.

Pri. After so many hours, lives, speeches spent,
Thus once again says Nestor from the Greeks:
'Deliver Helen, and all damage else,
As honour, loss of time, travail, expense,   4
Wounds, friends, and what else dear that is consum'd
In hot digestion of this cormorant war,
Shall be struck off.'   Hector, what say you to 't?

Hect. Though no man lesser fears the Greeks than
   I,   8
As far as toucheth my particular,
Yet, dread Priam,
There is no lady of more softer bowels,
More spongy to suck in the sense of fear,   12
More ready to cry out 'Who knows what follows?'
Than Hector is.   The wound of peace is surety,
Surety secure; but modest doubt is call'd
The beacon of the wise, the tent that searches   16
To th' bottom of the worst.   Let Helen go.
Since the first sword was drawn about this question,
Every tithe soul, 'mongst many thousand dismes,
Hath been as dear as Helen; I mean, of ours.   20
If we have lost so many tenths of ours,
To guard a thing not ours nor worth to us,
Had it our name, the value of one ten,
What merit's in that reason which denies   24

6 cormorant: *ravenous*
9 toucheth my particular: *concerns me personally*
14 surety: *feeling of security*
15 secure: *over-confident*
19, 20 Every . . . Helen; *cf. n.*   tithe: *tenth*   dismes: *tenth*
    men sacrificed
23 Had . . . name: *i.e. even if she were a Trojan*

16 tent; *cf. n.*

The yielding of her up?

   Tro.   Fie, fie, my brother!
Weigh you the worth and honour of a king
So great as our dread father in a scale
Of common ounces? Will you with counters sum   28
The past proportion of his infinite?
And buckle in a waist most fathomless
With spans and inches so diminutive
As fears and reasons? Fie, for godly shame!   32

   Hel. No marvel, though you bite so sharp at reasons,
You are so empty of them. Should not our father
Bear the great sway of his affairs with reasons,
Because your speech hath none that tells him so?   36

   Tro. You are for dreams and slumbers, brother
    priest;
You fur your gloves with reason. Here are your rea-
    sons:
You know an enemy intends you harm;
You know a sword employ'd is perilous,   40
And reason flies the object of all harm.
Who marvels then, when Helenus beholds
A Grecian and his sword, if he do set
The very wings of reason to his heels,   44
And fly like chidden Mercury from Jove,
Or like a star disorb'd? Nay, if we talk of reason,
Let's shut our gates and sleep. Manhood and honour
Should have hare-hearts, would they but fat their
    thoughts   48
With this cramm'd reason. Reason and respect
Make livers pale, and lustihood deject.

28 counters; *cf. n.*   29 *Cf. n.*
33 reasons; *cf. n.*   38 You . . . reason; *cf. n.*
45 chidden: *scolded; cf. n.*   Mercury: *the messenger of the gods*
46 disorb'd: *thrown out of its proper sphere*
48 hare-hearts: *hearts as timid as a hare's*   fat: *feed*
49 respect: *reflection, caution*
50 livers: *the supposed seat of passion and courage*   lustihood:
   lustiness, bodily vigor   deject: *dejected*

Hect. Brother, she is not worth what she doth cost
The holding.

Tro.   What's aught but as 'tis valu'd?   52

Hect. But value dwells not in particular will;
It holds his estimate and dignity
As well wherein 'tis precious of itself
As in the prizer. 'Tis mad idolatry   56
To make the service greater than the god;
And the will dotes that is inclinable
To what infectiously itself affects,
Without some image of th' affected merit.   60

Tro. I take to-day a wife, and my election
Is led on in the conduct of my will;
My will enkindled by mine eyes and ears,
Two traded pilots 'twixt the dangerous shores   64
Of will and judgment. How may I avoid,
Although my will distaste what it elected,
The wife I chose? There can be no evasion
To blench from this and to stand firm by honour.   68
We turn not back the silks upon the merchant
When we have soil'd them, nor the remainder viands
We do not throw in unrespective sieve
Because we now are full. It was thought meet   72
Paris should do some vengeance on the Greeks.
Your breath of full consent bellied his sails;
The seas and winds, old wranglers, took a truce
And did him service; he touch'd the ports desir'd,   76
And for an old aunt whom the Greeks held captive

---

52 The holding: *to hold*   53 particular will; *cf. n.*
54 estimate: *valuation*   dignity: *worth*
56 prizer: *person who values a thing*
58 dotes: *acts foolishly*   58-60 *Cf. n.*
62 in the conduct: *under the guidance*   61 election: *choice*
66 distaste: *dislike*   64 traded: *experienced*
70 soil'd; *cf. n.*   remainder: *left over* 67, 68 There . . . honour; *cf. n.*
71 unrespective: *that does not care what is put into it*
basket; *cf. n.*   72-79 It . . . morning; *cf. n.*   sieve
74 Your . . . consent: *the wind of your approbation*
75 wranglers: *adversaries*   76 touch'd: *landed at*

He brought a Grecian queen, whose youth and fresh-
    ness
Wrinkles Apollo's, and makes stale the morning.
Why keep we her? The Grecians keep our aunt.   80
Is she worth keeping? Why, she is a pearl,
Whose price hath launch'd above a thousand ships,
And turn'd crown'd kings to merchants.
If you'll avouch 'twas wisdom Paris went,—   84
As you must needs, for you all cried, 'Go, go,'—
If you'll confess he brought home noble prize,—
As you must needs, for you all clapp'd your hands,
And cried, 'Inestimable!'—why do you now   88
The issue of your proper wisdoms rate,
And do a deed that Fortune never did,
Beggar the estimation which you priz'd
Richer than sea and land? O! theft most base,   92
That we have stol'n what we do fear to keep!
But thieves unworthy of a thing so stol'n,
That in their country did them that disgrace
We fear to warrant in our native place.   96

    Cas. [*Within.*] Cry, Troyans, cry!
    Pri.   What noise? what shriek is this?
    Tro. 'Tis our mad sister. I do know her voice.
    Cas. [*Within.*] Cry, Troyans!
    Hect. It is Cassandra.   100

      Enter Cassandra [*raving*] *with her hair
            about her ears.*

    Cas. Cry, Troyans, cry! Lend me ten thousand eyes,
And I will fill them with prophetic tears.
    Hect. Peace, sister, peace!
    Cas. Virgins and boys, mid-age and wrinkled old, 104

Soft infancy, that nothing can but cry,
Add to my clamour! Let us pay betimes
A moiety of that mass of moan to come.
Cry, Troyans, cry! Practise your eyes with tears! 108
Troy must not be, nor goodly Ilion stand;
Our firebrand brother, Paris, burns us all.
Cry, Troyans, cry! A Helen and a woe!
Cry, cry! Troy burns, or else let Helen go. *Exit.* 112
    Hect. Now, youthful Troilus, do not these high
       strains
Of divination in our sister work
Some touches of remorse? Or is your blood
So madly hot that no discourse of reason,   116
Nor fear of bad success in a bad cause,
Can qualify the same?
    Tro.   Why, brother Hector,
We may not think the justness of each act
Such and no other than event doth form it,   120
Nor once deject the courage of our minds,
Because Cassandra's mad. Her brainsick raptures
Cannot distaste the goodness of a quarrel
Which hath our several honours all engag'd   124
To make it gracious. For my private part,
I am no more touch'd than all Priam's sons;
And Jove forbid there should be done amongst us
Such things as might offend the weakest spleen   128
To fight for and maintain.
    Par. Else might the world convince of levity
As well my undertakings as your counsels;
But I attest the gods, your full consent   132

107 moiety: *portion*   110 firebrand; *cf. n.*
116 discourse of reason: *faculty of reasoning*
117 success: *result*   118 qualify: *control, regulate*
120 event: *outcome*   121 deject: *depress*
122 raptures: *prophetic ecstasies*   123 distaste: *render distasteful*
125 gracious: *righteous*   128 weakest spleen: *dullest spirit*
130 convince: *convict*   132 attest: *call to witness*

Gave wings to my propension and cut off
All fears attending on so dire a project.
For what, alas, can these my single arms?
What propugnation is in one man's valour,　　　136
To stand the push and enmity of those
This quarrel would excite? Yet, I protest,
Were I alone to pass the difficulties,
And had as ample power as I have will,　　　140
Paris should ne'er retract what he hath done,
Nor faint in the pursuit.
　　Pri.　　　　　　　　Paris, you speak
Like one besotted on your sweet delights.
You have the honey still, but these the gall;　　　144
So to be valiant is no praise at all.
　　Par. Sir, I propose not merely to myself
The pleasures such a beauty brings with it;
But I would have the soil of her fair rape　　　148
Wip'd off, in honourable keeping her.
What treason were it to the ransack'd queen,
Disgrace to your great worths, and shame to me,
Now to deliver her possession up　　　152
On terms of base compulsion! Can it be
That so degenerate a strain as this
Should once set footing in your generous bosoms?
There's not the meanest spirit on our party　　　156
Without a heart to dare or sword to draw
When Helen is defended, nor none so noble
Whose life were ill bestow'd or death unfam'd
Where Helen is the subject. Then, I say,　　　160
Well may we fight for her, whom, we know well,

133 propension: *inclination*　　　136 propugnation: *power of defense*
137 stand the push: *withstand the attack*
139 pass: *pass through, undergo*　　　142 faint: *lose heart*
145 So: *in such a way*　　　148 soil: *stain*　　rape: *abduction*
150 were it: *it would be*　　ransack'd: *carried off, ravished*
152 her possession: *possession of her*
155 once: *for a moment*　　generous: *noble*　　　156 on: *of*

The world's large spaces cannot parallel.

   Hect. Paris and Troilus, you have both said well;
And on the cause and question now in hand   164
Have gloz'd, but superficially; not much
Unlike young men, whom Aristotle thought
Unfit to hear moral philosophy.
The reasons you allege do more conduce   168
To the hot passion of distemper'd blood
Than to make up a free determination
'Twixt right and wrong; for pleasure and revenge
Have ears more deaf than adders to the voice   172
Of any true decision.   Nature craves
All dues be render'd to their owners: now,
What nearer debt in all humanity
Than wife is to the husband? If this law   176
Of nature be corrupted through affection,
And that great minds, of partial indulgence
To their benumbed wills, resist the same;
There is a law in each well-order'd nation   180
To curb those raging appetites that are
Most disobedient and refractory.
If Helen, then, be wife to Sparta's king,
As it is known she is, these moral laws   184
Of nature, and of nation, speak aloud
To have her back return'd. Thus to persist
In doing wrong extenuates not wrong,
But makes it much more heavy. Hector's opinion   188
Is this, in way of truth; yet, ne'ertheless,
My spritely brethren, I propend to you
In resolution to keep Helen still;
For 'tis a cause that hath no mean dependence   192

165 gloz'd: *commented*   166, 167 Aristotle . . . philosophy; *cf. n.*
169 distemper'd: *disturbed, heated*   172 adders; *cf. n.*
177 affection: *inclination, appetite*   178 partial: *too great*
179 benumbed: *insensible to higher principle*
190 spritely: *high-spirited*   propend: *incline*

Upon our joint and several dignities.

   Tro. Why, there you touch'd the life of our design.
Were it not glory that we more affected
Than the performance of our heaving spleens,   196
I would not wish a drop of Troyan blood
Spent more in her defence.   But, worthy Hector,
She is a theme of honour and renown,
A spur to valiant and magnanimous deeds,   200
Whose present courage may beat down our foes,
And fame in time to come canonize us;
For, I presume, brave Hector would not lose
So rich advantage of a promis'd glory   204
As smiles upon the forehead of this action
For the wide world's revenue.

   Hect.   I am yours,
You valiant offspring of great Priamus.
I have a roisting challenge sent amongst   208
The dull and factious nobles of the Greeks
Will strike amazement to their drowsy spirits.
I was advertis'd their great general slept
Whilst emulation in the army crept.   212
This, I presume, will wake him.   *Exeunt.*

Scene Three

[*The Greek Camp.   Before Achilles' Tent*]

Enter Thersites solus.

   Ther. How now, Thersites!   What, lost in the
labyrinth of thy fury!   Shall the elephant Ajax
carry it thus?   He beats me, and I rail at him.
O worthy satisfaction!   Would it were otherwise;   4

---

196 heaving spleens: *rising passions*   201 Whose: *i.e. of the deeds*
202 canonize: *enrol among heroes*   208 roisting: *blustering*
210 amazement: *bewilderment*   211 advertis'd: *informed*
212 emulation: *jealous rivalry*   3 carry it: *behave*

that I could beat him, whilst he rail'd at me.
'Sfoot, I'll learn to conjure and raise devils, but
I'll see some issue of my spiteful execrations.
Then there's Achilles, a rare enginer. If Troy be 8
not taken till these two undermine it, the walls
will stand till they fall of themselves. O! thou
great thunder-darter of Olympus, forget that
thou art Jove, the king of gods, and, Mercury, 12
lose all the serpentine craft of thy caduceus, if
ye take not that little, little, less than little wit
from them that they have; which short-armed
ignorance itself knows is so abundant scarce it 16
will not in circumvention deliver a fly from a
spider, without drawing their massy irons and
cutting the web. After this, the vengeance on
the whole camp! or, rather, the [Neapolitan] 20
bone-ache! for that, methinks, is the curse dependent on those that war for a placket. I have
said my prayers, and devil Envy say Amen.
What, ho! my Lord Achilles!   24

Enter Patroclus.

Patr. Who's there? Thersites! Good Thersites, come in and rail.

Ther. If I could have remembered a gilt
counterfeit, thou wouldst not have slipped out 28
of my contemplation; but it is no matter; thyself upon thyself! The common curse of man-
kind, folly and ignorance, be thine in great
revenue! Heaven bless thee from a tutor, and 32

6 'Sfoot: *God's foot (a petty oath)*
8 enginer: *maker of military engines or works*
13 caduceus: *Mercury's wand*
15 short-armed: *i.e. having a short reach*   16 abundant: *extremely*
20 Neapolitan; *cf. n.*   22 placket: *i.e. the wearer of a petticoat*
27-29 *Cf. n.*   32 revenue: *abundance*   bless: *save*

discipline come not near thee! Let thy blood be
thy direction till thy death! Then, if she that
lays thee out says thou art a fair corse, I'll be
sworn and sworn upon 't she never shrouded 36
any but lazars. Amen. Where's Achilles?

Patr. What! art thou devout? Wast thou in
prayer?

Ther. Ay; the heavens hear me!   40

[*Patr.* Amen.]

Enter Achilles.

Achil. Who's there?

Patr. Thersites, my lord.

Achil. Where, where? Art thou come? Why, 44
my cheese, my digestion, why hast thou not
served thyself in to my table so many meals?
Come, what's Agamemnon?

Ther. Thy commander, Achilles. Then tell 48
me, Patroclus, what's Achilles?

Patr. Thy lord, Thersites. Then tell me, I
pray thee, what's thyself?

Ther. Thy knower, Patroclus. Then tell me, 52
Patroclus, what art thou?

Patr. Thou mayst tell that knowest.

Achil. O! tell, tell.

Ther. I'll decline the whole question. Aga- 56
memnon commands Achilles; Achilles is my lord;
I am Patroclus' knower; and Patroclus is a fool.

Patr. You rascal!

Ther. Peace, fool! I have not done.   60

Achil. He is a privileged man. Proceed,
Thersites.

33 blood: *passions, natural inclinations*   34 direction: *director*
35 corse: *corpse*   37 lazars: *lepers*   45 cheese; *cf. n.*
56 decline: *go through (as in a grammatical declension)*   question:
subject

Ther. Agamemnon is a fool; Achilles is a fool; Thersites is a fool; and, as aforesaid, 64 Patroclus is a fool.

Achil. Derive this; come.

Ther. Agamemnon is a fool to offer to command Achilles; Achilles is a fool to be com- 68 manded of Agamemnon; Thersites is a fool to serve such a fool; and Patroclus is a fool positive.

Patr. Why am I a fool? 72

Ther. Make that demand to the Creator. It suffices me thou art. Look you, who comes here?

Achil. Patroclus, I'll speak with nobody. 76 Come in with me, Thersites. *Exit.*

Ther. Here is such patchery, such juggling, and such knavery! All the argument is a cuckold and a whore; a good quarrel to draw 80 emulations, factions, and bleed to death upon. Now, the dry serpigo on the subject, and war and lechery confound all! [*Exit.*]

Enter Agamemnon, Ulysses, Nestor, Diomedes,
Ajax, and Calchas.

Agam. Where is Achilles? 84

Patr. Within his tent; but ill-dispos'd, my lord.

Agam. Let it be known to him that we are here.
He shent our messengers; and we lay by
Our appertainments, visiting of him. 88
Let him be told so, lest perchance he think
We dare not move the question of our place,

66 Derive: *trace the origin of* (*grammatical term*)
71 positive: *absolute*   78 patchery: *roguery*
79 argument: *subject matter*   82 serpigo: *skin eruption*
87 shent: *rebuked; cf. n.*   88 appertainments: *rights, prerogatives*
89 told . . . lest; *cf. n.*   90 *Cf. n.*

Or know not what we are.

    Patr.   I shall so say to him.

                                        [*Exit.*]

    Ulyss. We saw him at the opening of his tent.   92
He is not sick.

    Ajax. Yes, lion-sick, sick of proud heart. You
may call it melancholy if you will favour the
man; but, by my head, it is pride. But why, 96
why? Let him show us the cause. A word, my
lord.   [*Takes Agamemnon aside.*]

    Nest. What moves Ajax thus to bay at him?

    Ulyss. Achilles hath inveigled his fool from 100
him.

    Nest. Who, Thersites?

    Ulyss. He.

    Nest. Then will Ajax lack matter, if he have 104
lost his argument.

    Ulyss. No; you see, he is his argument that
has his argument, Achilles.

    Nest. All the better; their fraction is more 108
our wish than their faction. But it was a strong
counsel that a fool could disunite.

    Ulyss. The amity that wisdom knits not folly
may easily untie. Here comes Patroclus.   112

Enter Patroclus.

    Nest. No Achilles with him.

    Ulyss. The elephant hath joints, but none for
courtesy. His legs are legs for necessity, not for
flexure.   116

    Patr. Achilles bids me say, he is much sorry
If anything more than your sport and pleasure
Did move your greatness and this noble state

104-107 *Cf. n.*   108 fraction: *rupture*
114-116 *Cf. n.*   116 flexure: *bending*

To call upon him; he hopes it is no other   120
But, for your health and your digestion sake,
An after-dinner's breath.
    Agam.   Hear you, Patroclus.
We are too well acquainted with these answers;
But his evasion, wing'd thus swift with scorn,   124
Cannot outfly our apprehensions.
Much attribute he hath, and much the reason
Why we ascribe it to him; yet all his virtues,
Not virtuously of his own part beheld,   128
Do in our eyes begin to lose their gloss,
Yea, like fair fruit in an unwholesome dish,
Are like to rot untasted.   Go and tell him,
We came to speak with him; and you shall not sin 132
If you do say we think him over-proud
And under-honest, in self-assumption greater
Than in the note of judgment; and worthier than
    himself
Here tends the savage strangeness he puts on,   136
Disguise the holy strength of their command,
And underwrite in an observing kind
His humorous predominance; yea, watch
His pettish lines, his ebbs, his flows, as if   140
The passage and whole carriage of this action
Rode on his tide.   Go tell him this, and add,
That if he overhold his price so much,
We'll none of him; but let him, like an engine   144

122 breath: *exercise*   125 apprehensions: *understanding*
126 attribute: *credit, reputation*
128 Not virtuously: *i.e. arrogantly*
134 under-honest: *wanting in straightforwardness*
135 note of judgment; *cf. n.*
136 tends: *attend on*   savage strangeness: *rude aloofness*
138 underwrite: *submit to*   observing: *respectful*   kind: *way*
139 humorous predominance: *capricious assumption of superiority*
140 pettish: *ill-humored*   lines: *caprices, fits of temper; cf. n.*
141 passage: *course*   carriage: *conduct, execution*
142 Rode . . . tide: *depended on him*
143 overhold: *overestimate*   144 engine: *military machine*

Not portable, lie under this report:
'Bring action hither, this cannot go to war.'
A stirring dwarf we do allowance give
Before a sleeping giant. Tell him so.   148
    Patr. I shall; and bring his answer presently.
                                            [*Exit.*]
    Agam. In second voice we'll not be satisfied;
We come to speak with him. Ulysses, enter you.
                                    Exit Ulysses.
    Ajax. What is he more than another?   152
    Agam. No more than what he thinks he is.
    Ajax. Is he so much? Do you not think he
thinks himself a better man than I am?
    Agam. No question.   156
    Ajax. Will you subscribe his thought, and
say he is?
    Agam. No, noble Ajax; you are as strong,
as valiant, as wise, no less noble, much more 160
gentle, and altogether more tractable.
    Ajax. Why should a man be proud? How
doth pride grow? I know not what it is.
    Agam. Your mind is the clearer, Ajax, and 164
your virtues the fairer. He that is proud eats
up himself. Pride is his own glass, his own
trumpet, his own chronicle; and whatever
praises itself but in the deed, devours the deed 168
in the praise.
    Ajax. I do hate a proud man, as I hate the
engendering of toads.
    Nest. [*Aside.*] Yet he loves himself. Is 't not 172
strange?

145 lie under: *be subject to*
147 stirring: *active*   allowance: *approbation*
149 presently: *immediately*
150 In second voice: *by an intermediary*
157 subscribe: *endorse, assent to*
166 glass: *mirror*   168 but: *except*

Enter Ulysses.

Ulyss. Achilles will not to the field to-morrow.

Agam. What's his excuse?

Ulyss.   He doth rely on none,
But carries on the stream of his dispose   176
Without observance or respect of any,
In will peculiar and in self-admission.

Agam. Why will he not upon our fair request
Untent his person and share the air with us?   180

Ulyss. Things small as nothing, for request's sake
          only,
He makes important. Possess'd he is with greatness,
And speaks not to himself but with a pride
That quarrels at self-breath. Imagin'd worth   184
Holds in his blood such swoln and hot discourse,
That 'twixt his mental and his active parts
Kingdom'd Achilles in commotion rages
And batters 'gainst itself. What should I say?   188
He is so plaguy proud, that the death-tokens of it
Cry 'No recovery.'

Agam.   Let Ajax go to him.
Dear lord, go you and greet him in his tent:
'Tis said he holds you well, and will be led   192
At your request a little from himself.

Ulyss. O Agamemnon, let it not be so!
We'll consecrate the steps that Ajax makes
When they go from Achilles. Shall the proud lord 196
That bastes his arrogance with his own seam,
And never suffers matter of the world

176 dispose: *frame of mind*   177 *Cf. n.*
178 In will peculiar: *following his own way*   self-admission: *self-*
     approbation
181 for request's sake: *because they are asked for*
184 self-breath: *his own words*   worth; *cf. n.*
185 swoln: *inflated*
187 Kingdom'd Achilles: *Achilles, a kingdom in himself*
189 death-tokens; *cf. n.*   197 seam: *fat, grease*

Enter his thoughts, save such as do revolve
And ruminate himself, shall he be worshipp'd   200
Of that we hold an idol more than he?
No, this thrice-worthy and right valiant lord
Must not so stale his palm, nobly acquir'd;
Nor, by my will, assubjugate his merit,   204
As amply titled as Achilles' is,
By going to Achilles.
That were to enlard his fat-already pride,
And add more coals to Cancer when he burns   208
With entertaining great Hyperion.
This lord go to him! Jupiter forbid,
And say in thunder, 'Achilles go to him.'   211

   Nest. [*Aside.*] O! this is well. He rubs the vein of
     him.

   Dio. [*Aside.*] And how his silence drinks up this
     applause!

   Ajax. If I go to him, with my armed fist   216
I'll pash him o'er the face.

   Agam. O, no! you shall not go.

   Ajax. An a' be proud with me, I'll pheese his pride.
Let me go to him.   220

   Ulyss. Not for the worth that hangs upon our
     quarrel.

   Ajax. A paltry, insolent fellow!

   Nest. [*Aside.*] How he describes himself!

   Ajax. Can he not be sociable?   224

   Ulyss. [*Aside.*] The raven chides blackness.

   Ajax. I'll let his humours blood.

   Agam. [*Aside.*] He will be the physician
that should be the patient.   228

203 stale: *make common or cheap*   palm: *glory*
204 assubjugate: *debase*
207 enlard: *fatten*   fat-already: *already swollen*
208, 209 *Cf. n.*   212 vein: *mood*
217 pash: *smash, strike*   219 pheese: *beat, whip*
226 let . . . blood: *purge his humors by bleeding*

Ajax. An all men were o' my mind,—

Ulyss. [*Aside.*] Wit would be out of fashion.

Ajax. A' should not bear it so, a' should eat
swords first. Shall pride carry it?   232

Nest. [*Aside.*] An 't would, you'd carry half.

Ulyss. [*Aside.*] A' would have ten shares.

Ajax. I will knead him; I will make him supple.

Nest. [*Aside.*] He's not yet through warm. 236
Force him with praises; pour in, pour in; his
ambition is dry.

Ulyss. [*To Agamemnon.*] My lord, you feed too
much on this dislike.

Nest. Our noble general, do not do so.   240

Dio. You must prepare to fight without Achilles.

Ulyss. Why, 'tis this naming of him doth him harm.
Here is a man—but 'tis before his face;
I will be silent.

Nest.   Wherefore should you so?   244
He is not emulous, as Achilles is.

Ulyss. Know the whole world, he is as valiant.

Ajax. A whoreson dog, that shall palter thus
with us! Would he were a Troyan!   248

Nest. What a vice were it in Ajax now,—

Ulyss. If he were proud,—

Dio. Or covetous of praise,—

Ulyss. Ay, or surly borne,—   252

Dio. Or strange, or self-affected!

Ulyss. Thank the heavens, lord, thou art of sweet
composure;

Praise him that got thee, she that gave thee suck;
Fame be thy tutor, and thy parts of nature   256

234 *Cf. n.*   236 through: *thoroughly; cf. n.*
237 Force: *stuff, season*   245 emulous: *vain*
247 palter: *trifle*   253 strange: *aloof*   self-affected: *self-centred*
254 composure: *composition, temperament*
256 parts of nature: *natural qualities*

Thrice-fam'd, beyond all erudition;
But he that disciplin'd thy arms to fight,
Let Mars divide eternity in twain,
And give him half; and, for thy vigour,   260
Bull-bearing Milo his addition yield
To sinewy Ajax.   I will not praise thy wisdom,
Which, like a bourn, a pale, a shore, confines
Thy spacious and dilated parts.   Here's Nestor   264
Instructed by the antiquary times,
He must, he is, he cannot but be wise;
But pardon, father Nestor, were your days
As green as Ajax, and your brain so temper'd,   268
You should not have the eminence of him,
But be as Ajax.
 Ajax.   Shall I call you father?
 Ulyss. Ay, my good son.
 Dio.   Be rul'd by him, Lord Ajax.
 Ulyss. There is no tarrying here; the hart
  Achilles   272
Keeps thicket.   Please it our great general
To call together all his state of war;
Fresh kings are come to Troy; to-morrow,
We must with all our main of power stand fast;   276
And here's a lord,—come knights from east to west,
And cull their flower, Ajax shall cope the best.
 Agam. Go we to council. Let Achilles sleep:
Light boats sail swift, though greater hulks draw
  deep.   *Exeunt.* 280

261 Milo; *cf. n.* addition: *title, fame*
263 bourn: *boundary* pale: *paling, fence*
264 dilated: *spread far and wide*
265 antiquary: *rich in the lore of the past*
269 eminence: *advantage*   268 green: *youthful*
276 main of power: *whole body of troops* 274 state: *council*
278 cope: *match*
              280 boats sail; *cf. n.*

ACT THIRD

Scene One

[*Troy.   Before Priam's Palace*]

Music sounds within.   Enter Pandarus and a Servant.

Pan. Friend, you! pray you, a word.   Do not
you follow the young Lord Paris?

Serv. Ay, sir, when he goes before me.

Pan. You depend upon him, I mean?   4

Serv. Sir, I do depend upon the Lord.

Pan. You depend upon a noble gentleman;
I must needs praise him.

Serv. The Lord be praised!   8

Pan. You know me, do you not?

Serv. Faith, sir, superficially.

Pan. Friend, know me better.   I am the
Lord Pandarus.   12

Serv. I hope I shall know your honour
better.

Pan. I do desire it.

Serv. You are in the state of grace.   16

Pan. Grace!   Not so, friend.   Honour and
lordship   are   my   titles.   What   music   is
this?

Serv. I do but partly know, sir.   It is music 20
in parts.

Pan. Know you the musicians?

Serv. Wholly, sir.

Pan. Who play they to?   24

Serv. To the hearers, sir.

Pan. At whose pleasure, friend?

2 follow: *serve*   13-18 *Cf. n.*

Serv. At mine, sir, and theirs that love music.

Pan. Command, I mean, friend.   28

Serv. Who shall I command, sir?

Pan. Friend, we understand not one another. I am too courtly, and thou art too cunning. At whose request do these men play?   32

Serv. That's to 't, indeed, sir. Marry, sir, at the request of Paris, my lord, who's there in person; with him the mortal Venus, the heart-blood of beauty, love's invisible soul.   36

Pan. Who? My cousin Cressida?

Serv. No, sir, Helen. Could you not find out that by her attributes?

Pan. It should seem, fellow, that thou hast 40 not seen the Lady Cressida. I come to speak with Paris from the Prince Troilus. I will make a complimental assault upon him, for my business seethes.   44

Serv. Sodden business! There's a stewed phrase, indeed.

Enter Paris and Helen [attended].

Pan. Fair be to you, my lord, and to all this fair company! Fair desires, in all fair measure, 48 fairly guide them! especially to you, fair queen! Fair thoughts be your fair pillow!

Helen. Dear lord, you are full of fair words.

Pan. You speak your fair pleasure, sweet 52 queen. Fair prince, here is good broken music.

Par. You have broke it, cousin; and, by my life, you shall make it whole again; you shall

31 courtly: *refined in speech*
36 love's . . .soul; *cf. n.*
44 seethes: *is urgent*
53 broken music: *music in parts*
35, 36 heart-blood: *essence*
43 complimental: *courteous*
45, 46 stewed phrase; *cf. n.*

piece it out with a piece of your performance. 56
Nell, he is full of harmony.

Pan. Truly, lady, no.

Helen. O, sir!

Pan. Rude, in sooth; in good sooth, very 60
rude.

Par. Well said, my lord! Well, you say so
in fits.

Pan. I have business to my lord, dear queen. 64
My lord, will you vouchsafe me a word?

Helen. Nay, this shall not hedge us out.
We'll hear you sing, certainly.

Pan. Well, sweet queen, you are pleasant 68
with me. But, marry, thus, my lord. My dear
lord and most esteemed friend, your brother
Troilus—

Helen. My lord Pandarus, honey-sweet 72
lord,—

Pan. Go to, sweet queen, go to:—commends
himself most affectionately to you.

Helen. You shall not bob us out of our 76
melody. If you do, our melancholy upon your
head!

Pan. Sweet queen, sweet queen! That's a
sweet queen, i' faith.   80

Helen. And to make a sweet lady sad is a
sour offence.

Pan. Nay, that shall not serve your turn;
that shall it not, in truth, la! Nay, I care not 84
for such words; no, no. And, my lord, he
desires you, that if the king call for him at
supper, you will make his excuse.

Helen. My Lord Pandarus,—   88

Pan. What says my sweet queen, my very, very sweet queen?

Par. What exploit's in hand? Where sups he to-night?   92

Helen. Nay, but my lord,—

Pan. What says my sweet queen? My cousin will fall out with you.

Helen. You must not know where he sups.   96

Par. [I'll lay my life,] with my disposer Cressida.

Pan. No, no; no such matter; you are wide. Come, your disposer is sick.   100

Par. Well, I'll make excuse.

Pan. Ay, good my lord. Why should you say Cressida? No, your poor disposer's sick.

Par. I spy.   104

Pan. You spy! What do you spy? Come, give me an instrument now, sweet queen.

Helen. Why, this is kindly done.

Pan. My niece is horribly in love with a 108 thing you have, sweet queen.

Helen. She shall have it, my lord, if it be not my Lord Paris.

Pan. He! No, she'll none of him; they two 112 are twain.

Helen. Falling in, after falling out, may make them three.

Pan. Come, come, I'll hear no more of this. 116 I'll sing you a song now.

Helen. Ay, ay, prithee now. By my troth, sweet lord, thou hast a fine forehead.

Pan. Ay, you may, you may.   120

97 disposer; *cf. n.*
113 twain: *at variance*

99 wide: *i.e. of the mark*
119 fine forehead; *cf. n.*

Helen. Let thy song be love. This love will
undo us all. O Cupid, Cupid, Cupid!

Pan. Love! ay, that it shall, i' faith.

Par. Ay, good now, love, love, nothing but 124
love.

Pan. In good troth, it begins so:
[*Sings.*]
'Love, love, nothing but love, still more!
　　For, O! love's bow　　　　　　　　　　128
　　Shoots buck and doe.
　　The shaft confounds,
　　Not that it wounds,
But tickles still the sore.　　　　　　　　132
These lovers cry Oh! ho! they die!
　　Yet that which seems the wound to kill,
Doth turn Oh! ho! to ha! ha! he!
　　So dying love lives still:　　　　　　136
Oh! ho! a while, but ha! ha! ha!
Oh! ho! groans out for ha! ha! ha!'
Heigh-ho!

Helen. In love, i' faith, to the very tip of the 140
nose.

Par. He eats nothing but doves, love, and
that breeds hot blood, and hot blood begets hot
thoughts, and hot thoughts beget hot deeds, and 144
hot deeds is love.

Pan. Is this the generation of love,—hot
blood, hot thoughts, and hot deeds? Why,
they are vipers. Is love a generation of vipers? 148
Sweet lord, who's a-field to-day?

Par. Hector, Deiphobus, Helenus, Antenor,
and all the gallantry of Troy. I would fain have

130 confounds: *annoys*　　　　　　131 that: *i.e. because*
132 sore; *cf. n.*　　　　　　　　134 to kill: *which will kill*(?)

armed to-day, but my Nell would not have it so. 152
How chance my brother Troilus went not?

Helen. He hangs the lip at something. You
know all, Lord Pandarus.

Pan. Not I, honey-sweet queen. I long to 156
hear how they sped to-day. You'll remember
your brother's excuse?

Par. To a hair.

Pan. Farewell, sweet queen.   160

Helen. Commend me to your niece.

Pan. I will, sweet queen.

> [*Exit.*] *Sound a retreat.*

Par. They're come from field. Let us to Priam's
hall
To greet the warriors. Sweet Helen, I must woo
you   164
To help unarm our Hector. His stubborn buckles,
With these your white enchanting fingers touch'd,
Shall more obey than to the edge of steel
Or force of Greekish sinews. You shall do more   168
Than all the island kings,—disarm great Hector.

Helen. 'Twill make us proud to be his servant,
Paris;
Yea, what he shall receive of us in duty
Gives us more palm in beauty than we have,   172
Yea, overshines ourself.

Par. Sweet, above thought I love thee.   *Exeunt.*

157 sped: *fared*   169 island: *i.e. Greek*
172 more palm: *greater preëminence*   174 *Cf. n.*

Scene Two

[The Same.   Pandarus' Garden]

Enter Pandarus and Troilus' Man.

Pan. How now! where's thy master? at my
cousin Cressida's?

Man. No, sir; he stays for you to conduct him
thither.   4

Enter Troilus.

Pan. O, here he comes! How now, how now!

Tro. Sirrah, walk off.   *[Exit Man.]*

Pan. Have you seen my cousin?

Tro. No, Pandarus. I stalk about her door,   8
Like a strange soul upon the Stygian banks
Staying for waftage. O, be thou my Charon,
And give me swift transportance to those fields
Where I may wallow in the lily-beds   12
Propos'd for the deserver! O gentle Pandarus!
From Cupid's shoulder pluck his painted wings,
And fly with me to Cressid.

Pan. Walk here i' th' orchard. I'll bring her
straight.   *Exit Pandarus.* 16

Tro. I am giddy; expectation whirls me round.
Th' imaginary relish is so sweet
That it enchants my sense.   What will it be
When that the watery palates taste indeed   20
Love's thrice-repured nectar?   Death, I fear me,
Swooning destruction, or some joy too fine,
Too subtle, potent, and too sharp in sweetness
For the capacity of my ruder powers.   24
I fear it much; and I do fear besides

---

10 waftage: *passage*   Charon; *cf. n.*   13 Propos'd: *promised*
16 orchard: *garden*   straight: *immediately*   20 watery: *watering*
21 repured; *cf. n.*   24 ruder: *not sufficiently refined*

That I shall lose distinction in my joys,
As doth a battle, when they charge on heaps
The enemy flying.   28

Enter Pandarus.

Pan. She's making her ready; she'll come
straight; you must be witty now. She does so
blush, and fetches her wind so short, as if she
were frayed with a sprite. I'll fetch her. It is 32
the prettiest villain; she fetches her breath as
short as a new-ta'en sparrow.   *Exit Pand*[*arus*].
Tro. Even such a passion doth embrace my bosom.
My heart beats thicker than a feverous pulse,   36
And all my powers do their bestowing lose,
Like vassalage at unawares encount'ring
The eye of majesty.

Enter Pandarus and Cressida.

Pan. Come, come, what need you blush? 40
Shame's a baby. Here she is now; swear the
oaths now to her that you have sworn to me.
What! are you gone again? You must be watch'd
ere you be made tame, must you? Come your 44
ways, come your ways; an you draw backward,
we'll put you i' the fills. Why do you not speak
to her? Come, draw this curtain, and let's see
your picture. Alas the day, how loath you are 48
to offend daylight! An 'twere dark, you'd close
sooner. So, so; rub on, and kiss the mistress.
How now! a kiss in fee-farm! Build there, car-

---

26 distinction in: *discrimination between*   27 battle: *army*
30 be witty: *have your wits about you* (?)
31 fetches her wind: *breathes*
32 frayed: *frightened*   sprite: *spirit, ghost*   It: *she*
36 thicker: *faster*   37 bestowing: *proper functions*
38 vassalage: *vassals*   43 watch'd; *cf. n.*
46 fills: *shafts*   47 draw . . . curtain; *cf. n.*
50 rub . . . mistress; *cf.n.*   51 in fee-farm: *forever; cf. n.*

penter; the air is sweet.   Nay, you shall fight 52
your hearts out ere I part you.   The falcon as the
tercel, for all the ducks i' th' river.   Go to, go to.

Tro. You have bereft me of all words, lady.

Pan. Words pay no debts, give her deeds; 56
but she'll bereave you o' th' deeds too if she
call your activity in question.   What! billing
again?   Here's 'In witness whereof the parties
interchangeably'——Come in, come in.   I'll go 60
get a fire.   [*Exit.*]

Cres. Will you walk in, my lord?

Tro. O Cressida! how often have I wish'd
me thus!   64

Cres. Wish'd, my lord!   The gods grant,——O
my lord!

Tro. What should they grant?   What makes
this pretty abruption?   What too curious dreg 68
espies my sweet lady in the fountain of our love?

Cres. More dregs than water, if my fears
have eyes.

Tro. Fears make devils of cherubins; they 72
never see truly.

Cres. Blind fear, that seeing reason leads,
finds safer footing than blind reason stumbling
without fear.   To fear the worst oft cures the 76
worse.

Tro. O, let my lady apprehend no fear.   In all
Cupid's pageant there is presented no monster.

Cres. Nor nothing monstrous neither?   80

Tro. Nothing but our undertakings; when
we vow to weep seas, live in fire, eat rocks, tame
tigers, thinking it harder for our mistress to

53, 54 The . . . river; *cf. n.*
59, 60 'In . . . interchangeably'; *cf. n.*
68 abruption: *breaking off*   curious: *embarrassing, causing care*
79 pageant: *theatrical show*

devise imposition enough than for us to undergo 84
any difficulty imposed. This is the monstruosity
in love, lady, that the will is infinite, and the
execution confin'd; that the desire is boundless,
and the act a slave to limit.   88

Cres. They say all lovers swear more performance than they are able, and yet reserve
an ability that they never perform, vowing
more than the perfection of ten and discharging 92
less than the tenth part of one. They that have
the voice of lions and the act of hares, are they
not monsters?

Tro. Are there such? Such are not we. 96
Praise us as we are tasted, allow us as we prove;
our head shall go bare, till merit crown it. No
perfection in reversion shall have a praise in
present; we will not name desert before his 100
birth, and, being born, his addition shall be
humble. Few words to fair faith. Troilus shall
be such to Cressid, as what envy can say worst
shall be a mock for his truth, and what truth 104
can speak truest not truer than Troilus.

Cres. Will you walk in, my lord?

Enter Pandarus.

Pan. What! blushing still? Have you not
done talking yet?   108

Cres. Well, uncle, what folly I commit, I
dedicate to you.

Pan. I thank you for that. If my lord get
a boy of you, you'll give him me. Be true to 112
my lord; if he flinch, chide me for it.

85 monstruosity: *monstrous quality*
97 tasted: *tested*   allow: *give approbation*
99 reversion: *future possession*   103, 104 as . . . truth; *cf. n.*

Tro. You know now your hostages; your
uncle's word, and my firm faith.

Pan. Nay, I'll give my word for her too. 116
Our kindred, though they be long ere they are
wooed, they are constant being won. They are
burrs, I can tell you; they'll stick where they
are thrown. 120

Cres. Boldness comes to me now, and brings me
heart.
Prince Troilus, I have lov'd you night and day
For many weary months.

Tro. Why was my Cressid then so hard to win? 124

Cres. Hard to seem won; but I was won, my lord,
With the first glance that ever—pardon me:
If I confess much you will play the tyrant.
I love you now; but not, till now, so much 128
But I might master it. In faith, I lie;
My thoughts were like unbridled children, grown
Too headstrong for their mother. See, we fools!
Why have I blabb'd? Who shall be true to us 132
When we are so unsecret to ourselves?
But, though I lov'd you well, I woo'd you not;
And yet, good faith, I wish'd myself a man,
Or that we women had men's privilege 136
Of speaking first. Sweet, bid me hold my tongue,
For in this rapture I shall surely speak
The thing I shall repent. See, see! your silence,
Cunning in dumbness, from my weakness draws 140
My soul of counsel from me. Stop my mouth.

Tro. And shall, albeit sweet music issues thence.

Pan. Pretty, i' faith.

Cres. My lord, I do beseech you, pardon me; 144
'Twas not my purpose thus to beg a kiss.

---

121 heart: *courage*   140 Cunning; *cf. n.*
141 soul of counsel: *inmost secret*

I am asham'd. O heavens! what have I done?
For this time will I take my leave, my lord.
    Tro. Your leave, sweet Cressid?   148
      Pan. Leave! An you take leave till to-morrow
morning,—
    Cres. Pray you, content you.
    Tro.   What offends you, lady?
    Cres. Sir, mine own company.   152
    Tro. You cannot shun yourself.
    Cres. Let me go and try.
I have a kind of self resides with you;
But an unkind self, that itself will leave   156
To be another's fool. Where is my wit?
I would be gone. I speak I know not what.
    Tro. Well know they what they speak that speaks
      so wisely.
    Cres. Perchance, my lord, I show more craft than
      love,   160
And fell so roundly to a large confession,
To angle for your thoughts. But you are wise,
Or else you love not, for to be wise, and love,
Exceeds man's might; that dwells with gods above. 164
    Tro. O! that I thought it could be in a woman—
As, if it can, I will presume in you—
To feed for aye her lamp and flames of love;
To keep her constancy in plight and youth,   168
Outliving beauty's outward, with a mind
That doth renew swifter than blood decays;
Or that persuasion could but thus convince me,
That my integrity and truth to you   172
Might be affronted with the match and weight
Of such a winnow'd purity in love;
How were I then uplifted! But, alas!

161 roundly: *plainly*   large: *free*   168 in plight and youth; *cf. n.*
169 outward: *external form*   173 affronted: *confronted*

I am as true as truth's simplicity,   176
And simpler than the infancy of truth.
   Cres. In that I'll war with you.
   Tro.   O virtuous fight!
When right with right wars who shall be most right.
True swains in love shall in the world to come   180
Approve their truths by Troilus. When their rimes,
Full of protest, of oath, and big compare,
Wants similes, truth tir'd with iteration,
As true as steel, as plantage to the moon,   184
As sun to day, as turtle to her mate,
As iron to adamant, as earth to th' centre,
Yet, after all comparisons of truth,
As truth's authentic author to be cited,   188
'As true as Troilus' shall crown up the verse
And sanctify the numbers.
   Cres.   Prophet may you be!
If I be false, or swerve a hair from truth,
When time is old and hath forgot itself,   192
When waterdrops have worn the stones of Troy,
And blind oblivion swallow'd cities up,
And mighty states characterless are grated
To dusty nothing, yet let memory,   196
From false to false, among false maids in love
Upbraid my falsehood! When they've said, 'as false
As air, as water, as wind, as sandy earth,
As fox to lamb, as wolf to heifer's calf,   200
Pard to the hind, or stepdame to her son,'
Yea, let them say, to stick the heart of falsehood,
'As false as Cressid.'
    Pan. Go to, a bargain made; seal it, seal it; 204

181 Approve: *attest*
182 protest: *protestations*   big compare: *exaggerated comparisons*
184 plantage: *vegetation; cf. n.*   185 turtle: *turtle dove*
186 adamant: *loadstone*   189 crown up: *conclude*
190 numbers: *verses*   195 characterless: *unrecorded*
201 Pard: *leopard*   202 stick: *stab*

I'll be the witness.   Here I hold your hand, here
my cousin's.   If ever you prove false one to another, since I have taken such pains to bring you
together, let all pitiful goers-between be called to 208
the world's end after my name; call them all
Pandars; let all constant men be Troiluses, all
false women Cressids, and all brokers-between
Pandars! Say, Amen.   212

Tro. Amen.

Cres. Amen.

Pan. Amen. Whereupon I will show you a
chamber whose bed, because it shall not 216
speak of your pretty encounters, press it to
death.   Away!

And Cupid grant all tongue-tied maidens here
Bed, chamber, Pandar to provide this gear!   220

Exeunt.

Scene Three

[*The Greek Camp*]

*Enter Ulysses, Diomedes, Nestor, Agamemnon,
Menelaus, [Ajax,] and Calchas.*

Cal. Now, princes, for the service I have done you,
Th' advantage of the time prompts me aloud
To call for recompense. Appear it to your mind
That through the sight I bear in things to love,   4
I have abandon'd Troy, left my possession,
Incurr'd a traitor's name, expos'd myself,
From certain and possess'd conveniences,
To doubtful fortunes, sequest'ring from me all   8

215, 216 Whereupon . . . bed; *cf. n.*   217 press; *cf. n.*
2 advantage: *fitness*   aloud: *openly and forcibly*
4 *Cf. n.*   5 possession: *property*
7 conveniences: *advantages*   8 sequest'ring: *putting away*

That time, acquaintance, custom, and condition
Made tame and most familiar to my nature;
And here, to do you service, am become
As new into the world, strange, unacquainted.   12
I do beseech you, as in way of taste,
To give me now a little benefit,
Out of those many register'd in promise,
Which, you say, live to come in my behalf.   16
   Agam. What wouldst thou of us, Troyan? Make de-
     mand.
   Cal. You have a Troyan prisoner, call'd Antenor,
Yesterday took; Troy holds him very dear.
Oft have you—often have you thanks therefore—   20
Desir'd my Cressid in right great exchange,
Whom Troy hath still denied; but this Antenor
I know is such a wrest in their affairs
That their negotiations all must slack,   24
Wanting his manage; and they will almost
Give us a prince of blood, a son of Priam,
In change of him. Let him be sent, great princes,
And he shall buy my daughter; and her presence   28
Shall quite strike off all service I have done,
In most accepted pain.
   Agam.   Let Diomedes bear him,
And bring us Cressid hither. Calchas shall have
What he requests of us. Good Diomed,   32
Furnish you fairly for this interchange;
Withal bring word if Hector will to-morrow
Be answer'd in his challenge: Ajax is ready.

10 tame: *gentle*   12 new . . . world: *newly born*
13 taste: *foretaste*   14 benefit: *reward*
19 took: *taken*   20 have you thanks; *cf. n.*
21 in . . . exchange; *cf. n.*
23 wrest: *tuning-key, controlling influence*
25 Wanting: *lacking*   manage: *management*
27 change of: *exchange for*   30 In . . . pain; *cf. n.*
33 Furnish you: *equip yourself*

Dio. This shall I undertake; and 'tis a burthen   36
Which I am proud to bear.

            Exit [Diomedes, with Calchas].

Enter Achilles and Patroclus, in their tent.

Ulyss. Achilles stands i' th' entrance of his tent.
Please it our general to pass strangely by him,
As if he were forgot; and, princes all,   40
Lay negligent and loose regard upon him.
I will come last. 'Tis like he'll question me
Why such unplausive eyes are bent, why turn'd, on him.
If so, I have derision med'cinable   44
To use between your strangeness and his pride,
Which his own will shall have desire to drink.
It may do good; pride hath no other glass
To show itself but pride, for supple knees   48
Feed arrogance and are the proud man's fees.

Agam. We'll execute your purpose, and put on
A form of strangeness as we pass along.
So do each lord, and either greet him not,   52
Or else disdainfully, which shall shake him more
Than if not look'd on. I will lead the way.

Achil. What comes the general to speak with me?
You know my mind; I'll fight no more 'gainst Troy. 56

Agam. What says Achilles? Would he aught with
   us?

Nest. Would you, my lord, aught with the general?

Achil. No.

Nest. Nothing, my lord.   60

Agam. The better.

        [Exeunt Agamemnon and Nestor.]

Achil. Good day, good day.

Men. How do you? How do you?   *[Exit.]*

42 like: *probable*   43 unplausive: *unflattering*
48 show: *reflect*   50 put on: *assume*
51 form: *appearance*   55 What: *why*

Achil. What, does the cuckold scorn me?   64
Ajax. How now, Patroclus?
Achil. Good morrow, Ajax.
Ajax. Ha?
Achil. Good morrow.   68
Ajax. Ay, and good next day too.   [*Exit.*]
Achil. What mean these fellows? Know they not
    Achilles?
Patr. They pass by strangely. They were us'd to
    bend,
To send their smiles before them to Achilles,   72
To come as humbly as they us'd to creep
To holy altars.
  Achil.   What, am I poor of late?
'Tis certain, greatness, once fall'n out with fortune,
Must fall out with men too. What the declin'd is   76
He shall as soon read in the eyes of others
As feel in his own fall; for men, like butterflies,
Show not their mealy wings but to the summer,
And not a man, for being simply man,   80
Hath any honour, but honour'd for those honours
That are without him, as place, riches, and favour,
Prizes of accident as oft as merit;
Which when they fall, as being slippery standers,   84
The love that lean'd on them as slippery too,
Doth one pluck down another, and together
Die in the fall. But 'tis not so with me;
Fortune and I are friends. I do enjoy   88
At ample point all that I did possess,
Save these men's looks; who do, methinks, find out
Something not worth in me such rich beholding
As they have often given. Here is Ulysses;   92
I'll interrupt his reading.

76 declin'd: *man fallen from greatness*   82 without: *external to*
84-87 Which . . . fall; *cf. n.*   89 At ample point: *in full measure*

How now, Ulysses!
   Ulyss.   Now, great Thetis' son!
   Achil. What are you reading?
   Ulyss.   A strange fellow here
Writes me,
          'That man, how dearly ever parted,   96
How much in having, or without or in,
Cannot make boast to have that which he hath,
Nor feels not what he owes but by reflection;
As when his virtues shining upon others   100
Heat them, and they retort that heat again
To the first giver.'
   Achil.   This is not strange, Ulysses!
The beauty that is borne here in the face
The bearer knows not, but commends itself   104
[To others' eyes; nor doth the eye itself—
That most pure spirit of sense—behold itself,]
Not going from itself; but eye to eye oppos'd
Salutes each other with each other's form;   108
For speculation turns not to itself
Till it hath travell'd and is married there
Where it may see itself. This is not strange at all.
   Ulyss. I do not strain at the position,   112
It is familiar, but at the author's drift;
Who in his circumstance expressly proves
That no man is the lord of anything—
Though in and of him there is much consisting—   116
Till he communicate his parts to others;
Nor doth he of himself know them for aught

95 strange fellow; *cf. n.*
96 how . . . parted: *however richly endowed*
97 having: *possession*   or without or in: *in external possessions or
internal qualities*   99 owes: *owns*
101 retort: *throw back*   106 sense: *perception*
109 speculation: *power of sight*   110 married; *cf. n.*
112 strain: *doubt, cavil*   position: *thesis, assertion*
114 circumstance: *detailed argument*   116 consisting: *existing*
117 parts: *qualities*

Till he behold them formed in th' applause
Where they're extended; who, like an arch, rever-
　　b'rate   120
The voice again, or, like a gate of steel
Fronting the sun, receives and renders back
His figure and his heat.　I was much rapt in this;
And apprehended here immediately   124
The unknown Ajax.
Heavens, what a man is there!　A very horse,
That has he knows not what.　Nature, what things
　　there are,
Most abject in regard, and dear in use!   128
What things again most dear in the esteem
And poor in worth!　Now shall we see to-morrow,
An act that very chance doth throw upon him,
Ajax renown'd.　O heavens, what some men do,   132
While some men leave to do!
How some men creep in skittish Fortune's hall,
Whiles others play the idiots in her eyes!
How one man eats into another's pride,   136
While pride is feasting in his wantonness!
To see these Grecian lords!—why, even already
They clap the lubber Ajax on the shoulder,
As if his foot were on brave Hector's breast,   140
And great Troy shrinking.

　　Achil. I do believe it; for they pass'd by me
As misers do by beggars, neither gave to me
Good word nor look.　What, are my deeds forgot? 144

　　Ulyss. Time hath, my lord, a wallet at his back,
Wherein he puts alms for oblivion,
A great-siz'd monster of ingratitudes.

120　Where: *by which*　　　extended: *spread abroad*　　　who: *which*
　　arch: *vaulted roof*　　　　　123 figure: *appearance, reflection*
125　The unknown Ajax; *cf. n.*　　　　　126 very: *mere*
128　abject: *worthless, despicable*　regard: *estimation*　use: *utility*
133　leave: *fail*　　　　　　　　　　　　134, 135　*Cf. n.*
145　wallet: *sack*　　　　　　146 alms for oblivion; *cf. n.*

Those scraps are good deeds past, which are de-
    vour'd   148
As fast as they are made, forgot as soon
As done. Perseverance, dear my lord,
Keeps honour bright; to have done, is to hang
Quite out of fashion, like a rusty mail   152
In monumental mock'ry. Take the instant way;
For honour travels in a strait so narrow
Where one but goes abreast. Keep, then, the path;
For emulation hath a thousand sons   156
That one by one pursue. If you give way,
Or hedge aside from the direct forthright,
Like to an enter'd tide they all rush by
And leave you hindmost;   160
Or, like a gallant horse fall'n in first rank,
Lie there for pavement to the abject rear,
O'errun and trampled on. Then what they do in
    present,
Though less than yours in past, must o'ertop yours; 164
For time is like a fashionable host,
That slightly shakes his parting guest by th' hand,
And with his arms outstretch'd, as he would fly,
Grasps in the comer. The welcome ever smiles,   168
And farewell goes out sighing. O, let not virtue seek
Remuneration for the thing it was;
For beauty, wit,
High birth, vigour of bone, desert in service,   172
Love, friendship, charity, are subjects all
To envious and calumniating time.
One touch of nature makes the whole world kin,
That all with one consent praise new-born gawds, 176

152 mail: *suit of armor*
153 monumental: *memorial*   instant: *immediate*
154 strait: *narrow path*   155 one but: *only one*
158 hedge: *turn*   forthright: *straight path*
162 abject: *mean-spirited, despicable; cf. n.*
175 touch: *trait; cf. n.*   176 gawds: *gewgaws*

Though they are made and moulded of things past,
And give to dust that is a little gilt
More laud than gilt o'er-dusted.
The present eye praises the present object.   180
Then marvel not, thou great and complete man,
That all the Greeks begin to worship Ajax;
Since things in motion sooner catch the eye
Than what not stirs.   The cry went once on thee,   184
And still it might, and yet it may again,
If thou wouldst not entomb thyself alive,
And case thy reputation in thy tent;
Whose glorious deeds, but in these fields of late,   188
Made emulous missions 'mongst the gods themselves,
And drave great Mars to faction.
  Achil.   Of this my privacy
I have strong reasons.
  Ulyss.   But 'gainst your privacy
The reasons are more potent and heroical.   192
'Tis known, Achilles, that you are in love
With one of Priam's daughters.
  Achil. Ha! known!
  Ulyss. Is that a wonder?   196
The providence that's in a watchful state
Knows almost every grain of Pluto's gold,
Finds bottom in th' uncomprehensive deeps,
Keeps place with thought, and almost, like the gods, 200
Does thoughts unveil in their dumb cradles.
There is a mystery—with whom relation
Durst never meddle—in the soul of state,
Which hath an operation more divine   204

178 give; *cf. n.*
184 cry: *popular acclaim* once; *cf. n.*
189, 190 Made . . . faction; *cf. n.*
197 providence: *foresight*
199 uncomprehensive: *incomprehensible*
202 relation: *report, narration*

183 sooner; *cf. n.*
187 case: *shut up*
193, 194 *Cf. n.*
198 Pluto's; *cf. n.*
200, 201 *Cf. n.*
203 state: *statecraft*

Than breath or pen can give expressure to.
All the commerce that you have had with Troy
As perfectly is ours as yours, my lord;
And better would it fit Achilles much   208
To throw down Hector than Polyxena;
But it must grieve young Pyrrhus now at home,
When fame shall in our islands sound her trump,
And all the Greekish girls shall tripping sing,   212
'Great Hector's sister did Achilles win,
But our great Ajax bravely beat down him.'
Farewell, my lord; I as your lover speak;
The fool slides o'er the ice that you should break.   216
                                                        [*Exit.*]
   Patr. To this effect, Achilles, have I mov'd you.
A woman impudent and mannish grown
Is not more loath'd than an effeminate man
In time of action. I stand condemn'd for this.   220
They think my little stomach to the war
And your great love to me restrains you thus.
Sweet, rouse yourself; and the weak wanton Cupid
Shall from your neck unloose his amorous fold,   224
And, like a dew-drop from the lion's mane,
Be shook to airy air.
   Achil.   Shall Ajax fight with Hector?
   Patr. Ay; and perhaps receive much honour by him.
   Achil. I see my reputation is at stake;   228
My fame is shrewdly gor'd.
   Patr.   O, then, beware!
Those wounds heal ill that men do give themselves.
Omission to do what is necessary
Seals a commission to a blank of danger;   232

---

205 expressure: *expression*   207 ours: *i.e. known to us*
210 Pyrrhus: (*or Neoptolemus*) *the son of Achilles*
211 trump: *trumpet*   215 lover: *one devoted to you*
216 *Cf. n.*   217 mov'd: *spoken to*
229 shrewdly gor'd: *dangerously wounded; cf. n.*
232 *Cf. n.*

And danger, like an ague, subtly taints
Even then when we sit idly in the sun.

   Achil. Go call Thersites hither, sweet Patroclus.
I'll send the fool to Ajax and desire him   236
T' invite the Troyan lords after the combat
To see us here unarm'd. I have a woman's longing,
An appetite that I am sick withal,
To see great Hector in his weeds of peace,   240
To talk with him and to behold his visage,
Even to my full of view. A labour sav'd!

Enter Thersi[tes].

   Ther. A wonder!

   Achil. What?   244

   Ther. Ajax goes up and down the field, asking for himself.

   Achil. How so?

   Ther. He must fight singly to-morrow with 248
Hector, and is so prophetically proud of an
heroical cudgelling that he raves in saying
nothing.

   Achil. How can that be?   252

   Ther. Why, he stalks up and down like a
peacock,—a stride and a stand; ruminates like an
hostess that hath no arithmetic but her brain to
set down her reckoning; bites his lip with a 256
politic regard, as who should say 'There were wit
in this head, an 'twould out;' and so there is,
but it lies as coldly in him as fire in a flint, which
will not show without knocking. The man's 260
undone for ever, for if Hector break not his
neck i' th' combat, he'll break 't himself in vain-
glory. He knows not me. I said, 'Good morrow,

---

239 withal: *with*
242 full of view: *full satisfaction*
257 politic regard: *wise look*

240 weeds: *garments*
245, 246 *Cf. n.*

Ajax;' and he replies, 'Thanks, Agamemnon.' 264
What think you of this man that takes me for
the general? He's grown a very land-fish, lan-
guageless, a monster. A plague of opinion! A
man may wear it on both sides, like a leather 268
jerkin.

Achil. Thou must be my ambassador to him,
Thersites.

Ther. Who, I? Why, he'll answer nobody; he 272
professes not answering. Speaking is for beggars;
he wears his tongue in's arms. I will put on
his presence; let Patroclus make demands to me,
you shall see the pageant of Ajax.   276

Achil. To him, Patroclus. Tell him, I humbly
desire the valiant Ajax to invite the most valor-
ous Hector to come unarm'd to my tent, and to
procure safe-conduct for his person of the mag- 280
nanimous and most illustrious, six-or-seven-
times-honour'd captain, general of the Grecian
army, Agamemnon, et cætera. Do this.

Patr. Jove bless great Ajax!   284

Ther. Hum!

Patr. I come from the worthy Achilles,—

Ther. Ha!

Patr. Who most humbly desires you to in- 288
vite Hector to his tent,—

Ther. Hum!

Patr. And to procure safe-conduct from
Agamemnon.   292

Ther. Agamemnon?

Patr. Ay, my lord.

Ther. Ha!

Patr. What say you to 't?   296

267 opinion: *self-conceit*   273 professes: *makes a profession of*
274, 275 put . . . presence: *mimic him*

Ther. God buy you, with all my heart.

Patr. Your answer, sir.

Ther. If to-morrow be a fair day, by eleven o'clock it will go one way or other; howsoever, 300 he shall pay for me ere he has me.

Patr. Your answer, sir.

Ther. Fare you well, with all my heart.

Achil. Why, but he is not in this tune, is he?   304

Ther. No, but he's out o' tune thus. What music will be in him when Hector has knock'd out his brains, I know not; but, I am sure, none, unless the fiddler Apollo get his sinews to 308 make catlings on.

Achil. Come, thou shalt bear a letter to him straight.

Ther. Let me carry another to his horse, for 312 that's the more capable creature.

Achil. My mind is troubled, like a fountain stirr'd; And I myself see not the bottom of it.

     [*Exeunt Achilles and Patroclus.*]

Ther. Would the fountain of your mind were 316 clear again, that I might water an ass at it! I had rather be a tick in a sheep than such a valiant ignorance.   [*Exit.*]

297 buy: *be with*   309 catlings: *catgut strings*
313 capable: *intelligent*

ACT FOURTH

Scene One

[*Troy.   A Street*]

Enter, at one door, Æneas with a torch; at another,
*   Paris, Deiphobus, Antenor, Diomed the Grecian,*
*   [and others,] with torches.*

Par. See, ho! who is that there?
Dei.   It is the Lord Æneas.
Æne. Is the prince there in person?
Had I so good occasion to lie long
As you, Prince Paris, nothing but heavenly business 4
Should rob my bed-mate of my company.
Dio. That's my mind too.   Good morrow, Lord
    Æneas.
Par. A valiant Greek, Æneas; take his hand.
Witness the process of your speech, wherein   8
You told how Diomed, a whole week by days,
Did haunt you in the field.
Æne.   Health to you, valiant sir,
During all question of the gentle truce;
But when I meet you arm'd, as black defiance   12
As heart can think or courage execute.
Dio. The one and other Diomed embraces.
Our bloods are now in calm, and, so long, health!
But when contention and occasion meets,   16
By Jove, I'll play the hunter for thy life
With all my force, pursuit, and policy.
Æne. And thou shalt hunt a lion, that will fly
With his face backward.   In humane gentleness,   20

---

8 Witness . . . speech: *let the burden of your speech bear witness*
9 by days: *day by day*   11 question: *discussion*
16 *Cf. n.*

Welcome to Troy! Now, by Anchises' life,
Welcome, indeed! By Venus' hand I swear,
No man alive can love in such a sort
The thing he means to kill more excellently.   24
    Dio. We sympathize. Jove, let Æneas live,
If to my sword his fate be not the glory,
A thousand complete courses of the sun!
But, in mine emulous honour, let him die,   28
With every joint a wound, and that to-morrow!
    Æne. We know each other well.
    Dio. We do; and long to know each other worse.
    Par. This is the most despiteful'st gentle greet-
        ing,   32
The noblest hateful love, that e'er I heard of.
What business, lord, so early?
    Æne. I was sent for to the king; but why, I know
        not.
    Par. His purpose meets you; it was to bring this
        Greek   36
To Calchas' house, and there to render him,
For the enfreed Antenor, the fair Cressid.
Let's have your company; or, if you please,
Haste there before us. I constantly do think—   40
Or rather call my thought a certain knowledge—
My brother Troilus lodges there to-night.
Rouse him and give him note of our approach,
With the whole quality whereof. I fear   44
We shall be much unwelcome.
    Æne.   That I assure you.
Troilus had rather Troy were borne to Greece
Than Cressid borne from Troy.
    Par.   There is no help;

21 Anchises: *the father of Æneas*
23 sort: *manner*
33 hateful: *full of hate*
43 note: *notice*
                                    22 Venus' hand; *cf. n.*
                                    27 courses . . . sun: *years*
                                    40 constantly: *firmly*
                                    44 quality: *nature, circumstances*

The bitter disposition of the time   48
Will have it so.   On, lord; we'll follow you.
   Æne. Good morrow, all.   *Exit Æneas.*
   Par. And tell me, noble Diomed; faith, tell me true,
Even in the soul of sound good-fellowship,   52
Who, in your thoughts, merits fair Helen best—
Myself or Menelaus?
   Dio.   Both alike.
He merits well to have her that doth seek her,
Not making any scruple of her soilure,   56
With such a hell of pain and world of charge;
And you as well to keep her that defend her,
Not palating the taste of her dishonour,
With such a costly loss of wealth and friends.   60
He, like a puling cuckold, would drink up
The lees and dregs of a flat tamed piece;
You, like a lecher, out of whorish loins
Are pleas'd to breed out your inheritors.   64
Both merits pois'd, each weighs nor less nor more;
But he as he, which heavier for a whore.
   Par. You are too bitter to your countrywoman.
   Dio. She's bitter to her country.   Hear me, Paris: 68
For every false drop in her bawdy veins
A Grecian's life hath sunk; for every scruple
Of her contaminated carrion weight
A Troyan hath been slain.   Since she could speak, 72
She hath not given so many good words breath
As for her Greeks and Troyans suffer'd death.
   Par. Fair Diomed, you do as chapmen do,
Dispraise the thing that you desire to buy;   76
But we in silence hold this virtue well,

---

56 soilure: *defilement*   57 charge: *expense*
59 palating: *being sensible of*   62 tamed piece; *cf. n.*
65 pois'd: *weighed*   66 *Cf. n.*
75 chapmen: *merchants*

We'll not commend what we intend to sell.
Here lies our way.   *Exeunt.*

Scene Two

[The Same. A Court before Pandarus' House]

Enter Troilus and Cressida.

Tro. Dear, trouble not yourself; the morn is cold.
Cres. Then, sweet my lord, I'll call mine uncle down;
He shall unbolt the gates.
Tro.   Trouble him not;
To bed, to bed. Sleep kill those pretty eyes,   4
And give as soft attachment to thy senses
As infants' empty of all thought!
Cres.   Good morrow then.
Tro. I prithee now, to bed.
Cres.   Are you aweary of me?
Tro. O Cressida! but that the busy day,   8
Wak'd by the lark, hath rous'd the ribald crows,
And dreaming night will hide our eyes no longer,
I would not from thee.
Cres.   Night hath been too brief.
Tro. Beshrew the witch! with venomous wights she
      stays   12
As tediously as hell, but flies the grasps of love
With wings more momentary-swift than thought.
You will catch cold, and curse me.
Cres.   Prithee, tarry;
You men will never tarry.   16
O foolish Cressid! I might have still held off,
And then you would have tarried. Hark! there's one
      up.

---

78 *Cf. n.*   4 kill; *cf. n.*   5 attachment: *seizure*
12 venomous: *malignant*   13 tediously; *cf. n.*

Pan. (*Within.*) What, 's all the doors open here?
Tro. It is your uncle.   20
   Cres. A pestilence on him! Now will he be
mocking. I shall have such a life!

Enter Pandarus.

Pan. How now, how now! How go maidenheads?
Here, you maid, where's my cousin Cressid?   24
   Cres. Go hang yourself, you naughty mocking uncle!
You bring me to do—and then you flout me too.
   Pan. To do what? To do what? Let her say
what. What have I brought you to do?   28
   Cres. Come, come; beshrew your heart! You'll
      ne'er be good,
Nor suffer others.
   Pan. Ha, ha! Alas, poor wretch! A poor
capocchia! Hast not slept to-night? Would he 32
not, a naughty man, let it sleep? A bugbear take
him!
   Cres. Did not I tell you? would he were knock'd
i' th' head!   *One knocks.*
Who's that at door? Good uncle, go and see.   36
My lord, come you again into my chamber.
You smile, and mock me, as if I meant naughtily.
   Tro. Ha, ha!
   Cres. Come, you are deceiv'd, I think of no such
      thing.   *Knock.* 40
How earnestly they knock! Pray you, come in.
I would not for half Troy have you seen here.
                        Exeunt [*Troilus and Cressida*].
   Pan. Who's there? What's the matter? Will
you beat down the door? How now! what's 44
the matter?

26 flout: *mock*   30 suffer: *allow*   32 capocchia: *simpleton*

[Enter Æneas.]

Æne. Good morrow, lord, good morrow.

Pan. Who's there? My Lord Æneas! By my troth,
I knew you not. What news with you so early?   48

Æne. Is not Prince Troilus here?

Pan. Here? What should he do here?

   Æne. Come, he is here, my lord. Do not
deny him. It doth import him much to speak 52
with me.

   Pan. Is he here, say you? 'Tis more than
I know, I'll be sworn. For my own part, I came
in late. What should he do here?   56

   Æne. Who! nay, then. Come, come, you'll
do him wrong ere you're ware. You'll be so
true to him, to be false to him. Do not you know
of him, but yet go fetch him hither; go.   60

Enter Troilus.

Tro. How now! what's the matter?

Æne. My lord, I scarce have leisure to salute you,
My matter is so rash. There is at hand
Paris your brother, and Deiphobus,   64
The Grecian Diomed, and our Antenor
Deliver'd to us; and for him forthwith,
Ere the first sacrifice, within this hour,
We must give up to Diomedes' hand   68
The Lady Cressida.

   Tro.   Is it concluded so?

Æne. By Priam, and the general state of Troy.
They are at hand and ready to effect it.

   Tro. How my achievements mock me!   72
I will go meet them; and, my Lord Æneas,
We met by chance; you did not find me here.

52 import: *concern*   63 rash: *urgent*
69 concluded: *determined*

Æne..Good, good, my lord; the secrets of nature
Have not more gift in taciturnity.   76
                    Exeunt [*Troilus and Æneas*].

Pan. Is 't possible? No sooner got but lost?
The devil take Antenor! The young prince will
go mad. A plague upon Antenor! I would they
had broke 's neck!   80

Enter Cressid.

Cres. How now! What's the matter? Who
was here?

Pan. Ah! ha!

Cres. Why sigh you so profoundly? Where's 84
my lord? Gone? Tell me, sweet uncle, what's
the matter?

Pan. Would I were as deep under the earth
as I am above!   88

Cres. O the gods! what's the matter?

Pan. Prithee, get thee in. Would thou hadst
ne'er been born! I knew thou wouldst be his
death. O poor gentleman! A plague upon 92
Antenor!

Cres. Good uncle, I beseech you, on my
knees I beseech you, what's the matter?

Pan. Thou must be gone, wench, thou must 96
be gone; thou art chang'd for Antenor. Thou
must to thy father, and be gone from Troilus.
'Twill be his death; 'twill be his bane; he cannot
bear it.   100

Cres. O you immortal gods! I will not go.

Pan. Thou must.

Cres. I will not, uncle. I have forgot my father;
I know no touch of consanguinity;   104
No kin, no love, no blood, no soul so near me

99 bane: *death*   104 touch: *feeling*

As the sweet Troilus. O you gods divine!
Make Cressid's name the very crown of falsehood
If ever she leave Troilus! Time, force, and death, 108
Do to this body what extremes you can;
But the strong base and building of my love
Is as the very centre of the earth,
Drawing all things to it. I will go in and weep.   112

    Pan. Do, do.

    Cres. Tear my bright hair, and scratch my praised
      cheeks,
Crack my clear voice with sobs, and break my heart
With sounding Troilus. I will not go from Troy. 116
                               Exeunt.

Scene Three

[*The Same. Before Pandarus' House*]

*Enter Paris, Troilus, Æneas, Deiphobus, Antenor,
and Diomedes.*

    Par. It is great morning, and the hour prefix'd
Of her delivery to this valiant Greek
Comes fast upon. Good my brother Troilus,
Tell you the lady what she is to do,   4
And haste her to the purpose.

    Tro.   Walk into her house;
I'll bring her to the Grecian presently;
And to his hand when I deliver her,
Think it an altar, and thy brother Troilus   8
A priest, there offering to it his [own] heart. [*Exit.*]

    Par. I know what 'tis to love;
And would, as I shall pity, I could help!
Please you walk in, my lords.   *Exeunt.* 12

109 extremes; *cf. n.*   1 great morning: *broad daylight*
3 upon: *i.e. upon us*   11 *Cf. n.*

Scene Four

[*The Same.   A Room in Pandarus' House*]

Enter Pandarus and Cressid.

Pan. Be moderate, be moderate.
Cres. Why tell you me of moderation?
The grief is fine, full, perfect, that I taste,
And violenteth in a sense as strong   4
As that which causeth it.   How can I moderate it?
If I could temporize with my affection,
Or brew it to a weak and colder palate,
The like allayment could I give my grief.   8
My love admits no qualifying dross;
No more my grief, in such a precious loss.

Enter Troilus.

Pan. Here, here, here he comes.   A sweet duck!
Cres. [*Embracing him.*] O Troilus! Troilus!   12
Pan. What a pair of spectacles is here!   Let
me embrace too.   'O heart,' as the goodly saying is,—

    'O heart, heavy heart,   16
      Why sigh'st thou without breaking?'

where he answers again,

    'Because thou canst not ease thy smart
      By friendship nor by speaking.'   20

There was never a truer rime.   Let us cast away
nothing, for we may live to have need of such a
verse.   We see it, we see it.   How now, lambs!
Tro. Cressid, I love thee in so strain'd a purity,   24

4 violenteth: *rages; cf. n.*   7 palate: *taste*
19 smart: *pain*   24 strain'd; *cf. n.*

That the bless'd gods, as angry with my fancy,
More bright in zeal than the devotion which
Cold lips blow to their deities, take thee from me.

    Cres. Have the gods envy?   28

    Pan. Ay, ay, ay, ay; 'tis too plain a case.

    Cres. And is it true that I must go from Troy?

    Tro. A hateful truth.

    Cres.   What! and from Troilus too?

    Tro. From Troy and Troilus.

    Cres.   Is 't possible?   32

    Tro. And suddenly, where injury of chance
Puts back leave-taking, justles roughly by
All time of pause, rudely beguiles our lips
Of all rejoindure, forcibly prevents   36
Our lock'd embrasures, strangles our dear vows
Even in the birth of our own labouring breath.
We two, that with so many thousand sighs
Did buy each other, must poorly sell ourselves   40
With the rude brevity and discharge of one.
Injurious time now with a robber's haste
Crams his rich thievery up, he knows not how.
As many farewells as be stars in heaven,   44
With distinct breath and consign'd kisses to them,
He fumbles up into a loose adieu,
And scants us with a single famish'd kiss,
Distasting with the salt of broken tears.   48

    Æne. [*Within.*] My lord, is the lady ready?

    Tro. Hark! you are call'd. Some say the Genius so
Cries 'Come!' to him that instantly must die.
Bid them have patience; she shall come anon.   52

25 fancy: *love*   33 injury of chance: *ill usage by Fortune*
36 rejoindure: *meeting again*   prevents: *forestalls, precludes*
37 embrasures: *embraces*
43 thievery: *booty*   he . . . how: *in careless haste*
45 Cf. n.   47 scants: *treats in a niggardly way*
50 Genius; cf. n.

 Pan. Where are my tears? Rain, to lay this
wind, or my heart will be blown up by the root!

             [*Exit.*]

 Cres. I must, then, to the Grecians?

 Tro.   No remedy.

 Cres. A woeful Cressid 'mongst the merry Greeks! 56
When shall we see again?

 Tro. Hear me, my love. Be thou but true of heart,—

 Cres. I true! How now! What wicked deem is this?

 Tro. Nay, we must use expostulation kindly, 60
For it is parting from us.
I speak not 'be thou true,' as fearing thee,
For I will throw my glove to Death himself,
That there's no maculation in thy heart;   64
But, 'be thou true,' say I, to fashion in
My sequent protestation; be thou true,
And I will see thee.

 Cres. O! you shall be expos'd, my lord, to dangers 68
As infinite as imminent; but I'll be true.

 Tro. And I'll grow friend with danger. Wear this
  sleeve.

 Cres. And you this glove. When shall I see you?

 Tro. I will corrupt the Grecian sentinels, 72
To give thee nightly visitation.
But yet, be true.

 Cres.   O heavens! 'be true' again!

 Tro. Hear why I speak it, love.
The Grecian youths are full of quality;   76
They're loving, well compos'd, with gift of nature,
Flowing and swelling o'er with arts and exercise.

57 see: *i.e. each other; cf. n.*   59 deem: *thought*
60, 61 *Cf. n.*   62 fearing: *doubting*
63, 64 *Cf. n.*   64 maculation: *stain*
65, 66 to . . . protestation; *cf. n.* 76 full of quality: *richly gifted*
77, 78 *Cf. n.*
78 arts: *theoretical knowledge* exercise: *practical skill*

How novelties may move, and parts with person,
Alas! a kind of godly jealousy,—   80
Which, I beseech you, call a virtuous sin,—
Makes me afraid.

    Cres.   O heavens! you love me not.

    Tro. Die I a villain, then!
In this I do not call your faith in question   84
So mainly as my merit. I cannot sing,
Nor heel the high lavolt, nor sweeten talk,
Nor play at subtle games; fair virtues all,
To which the Grecians are most prompt and preg-
       nant;   88
But I can tell that in each grace of these
There lurks a still and dumb-discoursive devil
That tempts most cunningly. But be not tempted.

    Cres. Do you think I will?   92

    Tro. No.
But something may be done that we will not;
And sometimes we are devils to ourselves
When we will tempt the frailty of our powers,   96
Presuming on their changeful potency.

    Æne. (*Within.*) Nay, good my lord,—

    Tro.   Come, kiss; and let us part.

    Par. (*Within.*) Brother Troilus!

    Tro.   Good brother, come you hither;
And bring Æneas and the Grecian with you.   100

    Cres. My lord, will you be true?

    Tro. Who? I? Alas, it is my vice, my fault.
Whiles others fish with craft for great opinion,
I with great truth catch mere simplicity;   104
Whilst some with cunning gild their copper crowns,
With truth and plainness I do wear mine bare.

79 person: *attractive appearance*
86 lavolt: *a dance; cf. n.*
90 dumb-discoursive: *inaudibly speaking*
94 will: *intend*

84 in question: *in doubt*
88 pregnant: *naturally addicted*

103, 104 *Cf. n.*

Fear not my truth; the moral of my wit
Is 'plain and true'; there's all the reach of it.   108

> *Enter the Greeks [i.e. Æneas, Paris, Antenor,*
> *Deiphobus, and Diomedes].*

Welcome, Sir Diomed! Here is the lady
Which for Antenor we deliver you.
At the port, lord, I'll give her to thy hand,
And by the way possess thee what she is.   112
Entreat her fair; and, by my soul, fair Greek,
If e'er thou stand at mercy of my sword,
Name Cressid, and thy life shall be as safe
As Priam is in Ilion.

   Dio.   Fair Lady Cressid,   116
So please you, save the thanks this prince expects.
The lustre in your eye, heaven in your cheek,
Pleads your fair usage; and to Diomed
You shall be mistress, and command him wholly.   120
   Tro. Grecian, thou dost not use me courteously,
To shame the zeal of my petition to thee
In praising her. I tell thee, lord of Greece,
She is as far high-soaring o'er thy praises   124
As thou unworthy to be call'd her servant.
I charge thee use her well, even for my charge;
For, by the dreadful Pluto, if thou dost not,
Though the great bulk Achilles be thy guard,   128
I'll cut thy throat.
   Dio.   O! be not mov'd, Prince Troilus.
Let me be privileg'd by my place and message
To be a speaker free; when I am hence,
I'll answer to my lust; and know, my lord,   132

107 moral: *motto*   111 port: *gate*
112 by: *on*   possess: *inform*   what: *what sort of person*
113 Entreat: *treat*   122, 123 To . . . her; *cf. n.*
126 even . . . charge: *because I bid you do it*
132 answer . . . lust: *do as I please; cf. n.*

I'll nothing do on charge.   To her own worth
She shall be priz'd; but that you say 'be 't so,'
I'll speak it in my spirit and honour, 'no.'

   Tro. Come, to the port.   I'll tell thee, Diomed,   136
This brave shall oft make thee to hide thy head.
Lady, give me your hand, and, as we walk,
To our own selves bend we our needful talk.

> [*Exeunt Troilus, Cressida, and Diomedes.*]
> *Sound trumpet.*

   Par. Hark! Hector's trumpet.

   Æne.   How have we spent this morning! 140
The prince must think me tardy and remiss,
That swore to ride before him in the field.

   Par. 'Tis Troilus' fault.   Come, come, to field with
him.

   Dei. Let us make ready straight.   144

   Æne. Yea, with a bridegroom's fresh alacrity,
Let us address to tend on Hector's heels.
The glory of our Troy doth this day lie
On his fair worth and single chivalry.   *Exeunt.* 148

Scene Five

[*The Greek Camp. Lists set out*]

*Enter Ajax, armed; Achilles, Patroclus, Agamem-
non, Menelaus, Ulysses, Nestor, Calchas, &c.*

   Agam. Here art thou in appointment fresh and fair,
Anticipating time.   With starting courage,
Give with thy trumpet a loud note to Troy,
Thou dreadful Ajax; that the appalled air   4
May pierce the head of the great combatant

---

137 brave: *piece of bravado*   146 address: *prepare*
1 appointment: *equipment*   2 starting: *startling*

And hale him hither.

Ajax.   Thou, trumpet, there's my purse.
Now crack thy lungs, and split thy brazen pipe.
Blow, villain, till thy sphered bias cheek   8
Outswell the colic of puff'd Aquilon.
Come, stretch thy chest, and let thy eyes spout blood;
Thou blow'st for Hector.   [*Trumpet sounds.*]

   Ulyss. No trumpet answers.

   Achil.   'Tis but early days. 12

   Agam. Is not yond Diomed with Calchas' daughter?

   Ulyss. 'Tis he, I ken the manner of his gait;
He rises on the toe.   That spirit of his
In aspiration lifts him from the earth.   16

       [*Enter Diomedes, with Cressida.*]

   Agam. Is this the Lady Cressid?

   Dio.   Even she.

   Agam. Most dearly welcome to the Greeks, sweet
lady.

   Nest. Our general doth salute you with a kiss.

   Ulyss. Yet is the kindness put particular.   20
'Twere better she were kiss'd in general.

   Nest. And very courtly counsel.   I'll begin.
So much for Nestor.

   Achil. I'll take that winter from your lips, fair
lady.   24
Achilles bids you welcome.

   Men. I had good argument for kissing once.

   Patr. But that's no argument for kissing now;
For thus popp'd Paris in his hardiment,   28
[And parted thus you and your argument.]

6 hale: *draw*   trumpet: *trumpeter*   8 bias: *puffed out; cf. n.*
9 Aquilon: *the north wind*   11 for: *i.e. to summon*
12 days: *in the day*   14 ken: *know*
20 particular: *individual (with a quibble on the word 'general')*
26 argument: *reason*   28 hardiment: *boldness*

Ulyss. O, deadly gall, and theme of all our scorns!
For which we lose our heads to gild his horns.

Patr. The first was Menelaus' kiss; this, mine: 32
Patroclus kisses you.

Men.   O! this is trim.

Patr. Paris and I kiss evermore for him.

Men. I'll have my kiss, sir.   Lady, by your leave.

Cres. In kissing, do you render or receive?   36

Patr. Both take and give.

Cres.   I'll make my match to live,
The kiss you take is better than you give;
Therefore no kiss.

Men. I'll give you boot; I'll give you three for
   one.   40

Cres. You are an odd man; give even, or give none.

Men. An odd man, lady? Every man is odd.

Cres. No, Paris is not; for, you know 'tis true,
That you are odd, and he is even with you.   44

Men. You fillip me o' th' head.

Cres.   No, I'll be sworn.

Ulyss. It were no match, your nail against his horn.
May I, sweet lady, beg a kiss of you?

Cres. You may.

Ulyss.   I do desire it.

Cres.   Why, beg, then.   48

Ulyss. Why, then, for Venus' sake, give me a kiss,
When Helen is a maid again, and his—

Cres. I am your debtor; claim it when 'tis due.

Ulyss. Never's my day, and then a kiss of you.   52

Dio. Lady, a word.   I'll bring you to your father.
                    [*Diomedes leads out Cressida.*]

Nest. A woman of quick sense.

31 horns: *i.e. the horns of a cuckold*
37 I'll . . . live: *I'll wager my life*
40 boot: *odds*   45 fillip: *tap*

Ulyss.   Fie, fie upon her!
There's a language in her eye, her cheek, her lip,
Nay, her foot speaks; her wanton spirits look out   56
At every joint and motive of her body.
O, these encounterers, so glib of tongue,
That give a coasting welcome ere it comes,
And wide unclasp the tables of their thoughts   60
To every tickling reader! set them down
For sluttish spoils of opportunity
And daughters of the game.
      All. The Troyans' trumpet.
      Agam.   Yonder comes the troop. 64

Enter all of Troy, Hector [armed], Paris, Æneas,
     Helenus, [Troilus], and Attendants. Flourish.

      Æne. Hail, all you state of Greece;   What shall be
            done
To him that victory commands?   Or do you purpose
A victor shall be known?   Will you the knights
Shall to the edge of all extremity   68
Pursue each other, or shall be divided
By any voice or order of the field?
Hector bade ask.
      Agam.   Which way would Hector have it?
      Æne. He cares not; he'll obey conditions.   72
      Achil. 'Tis done like Hector; but securely done,
A little proudly, and great deal misprising
The knight oppos'd.
      Æne.   If not Achilles, sir,
What is your name?
      Achil.   If not Achilles, nothing.   76
      Æne. Therefore Achilles; but, whate'er, know this:

57 motive: *limb*   58 encounterers: *those who meet others halfway*
59 coasting: *sidelong, alluring*(?); *cf. n.*
60 tables: *tablets*   61 tickling: *prurient*
62 *Cf. n.*   74 misprising: *undervaluing*

In the extremity of great and little,
Valour and pride excel themselves in Hector;
The one almost as infinite as all,   80
The other blank as nothing. Weigh him well,
And that which looks like pride is courtesy.
This Ajax is half made of Hector's blood,
In love whereof half Hector stays at home;   84
Half heart, half hand, half Hector comes to seek
This blended knight, half Troyan, and half Greek.
    Achil. A maiden battle, then? O, I perceive you.

                    [*Enter Diomedes.*]

    Agam. Here is Sir Diomed. Go, gentle knight, 88
Stand by our Ajax. As you and Lord Æneas
Consent upon the order of their fight,
So be it; either to the uttermost,
Or else a breath. The combatants being kin   92
Half stints their strife before their strokes begin.
                [*Ajax and Hector enter the lists.*]
    Ulyss. They are oppos'd already.
    Agam. What Troyan is that same that looks so
        heavy?
    Ulyss. The youngest son of Priam, a true knight, 96
Not yet mature, yet matchless, firm of word,
Speaking in deeds and deedless in his tongue;
Not soon provok'd, nor being provok'd soon calm'd;
His heart and hand both open and both free;   100
For what he has he gives, what thinks, he shows;
Yet gives he not till judgment guide his bounty,
Nor dignifies an impair thought with breath;
Manly as Hector, but more dangerous;   104

78-81 In . . . nothing; *cf. n.*
87 maiden: *bloodless, like that of a novice*
95 heavy: *downcast*   90 Consent: *agree*
98 deedless . . . tongue: *i.e. not boastful*   96 *Cf. n.*
100 free: *noble, generous*
                                               103 impair: *unsuitable*

For Hector, in his blaze of wrath, subscribes
To tender objects, but he in heat of action
Is more vindicative than jealous love.
They call him Troilus, and on him erect   108
A second hope, as fairly built as Hector.
Thus says Æneas, one that knows the youth
Even to his inches, and with private soul
Did in great Ilion thus translate him to me.   112

     Alarum. [Hector and Ajax fight.]

Agam. They are in action.

Nest. Now, Ajax, hold thine own!

Tro.   Hector, thou sleep'st; awake thee!

Agam. His blows are well dispos'd.   There, Ajax!

Dio. You must no more.   *Trumpets cease.*

Æne.   Princes, enough, so please you. 116

Ajax. I am not warm yet; let us fight again.

Dio. As Hector pleases.

Hect.   Why, then will I no more.
Thou art, great lord, my father's sister's son,
A cousin-german to great Priam's seed;   120
The obligation of our blood forbids
A gory emulation 'twixt us twain.
Were thy commixtion Greek and Troyan so
That thou couldst say, 'This hand is Grecian all,   124
And this is Troyan; the sinews of this leg
All Greek, and this all Troy; my mother's blood
Runs on the dexter cheek, and this sinister
Bounds in my father's,' by Jove multipotent,   128
Thou shouldst not bear from me a Greekish member
Wherein my sword had not impressure made
Of our rank feud.   But the just gods gainsay

105, 106 in . . . objects; *cf. n.*
111 Even . . .inches: *from top to toe*
 his personal opinion
123 commixtion: *mixture (of blood)*
127 dexter: *right*   sinister: *left*
128 multipotent: *mighty*

107 vindicative: *vengeful*
 with . . . soul: *i.e. giving me*
112 translate: *explain, interpret*

130 impressure: *impression*

That any drop thou borrow'dst from thy mother,   132
My sacred aunt, should by my mortal sword
Be drain'd! Let me embrace thee, Ajax;
By him that thunders, thou hast lusty arms;
Hector would have them fall upon him thus.   136
Cousin, all honour to thee!

   Ajax.   I thank thee, Hector.
Thou art too gentle and too free a man.
I came to kill thee, cousin, and bear hence
A great addition earned in thy death.   140

   Hect. Not Neoptolemus so mirable,
On whose bright crest Fame with her loud'st Oyes
Cries, 'This is he!' could promise to himself
A thought of added honour torn from Hector.   144

   Æne. There is expectance here from both the sides,
What further you will do.

   Hect.   We'll answer it;
The issue is embracement. Ajax, farewell.

   Ajax. If I might in entreaties find success,—   148
As seld I have the chance,—I would desire
My famous cousin to our Grecian tents.

   Dio. 'Tis Agamemnon's wish, and great Achilles
Doth long to see unarm'd the valiant Hector.   152

   Hect. Æneas, call my brother Troilus to me,
And signify this loving interview
To the expecters of our Troyan part.
Desire them home. Give me thy hand, my cousin;   156
I will go eat with thee and see your knights.

      Agamemnon and the rest [*come forward*].

   Ajax. Great Agamemnon comes to meet us here.

   Hect. The worthiest of them tell me name by name;
But for Achilles, mine own searching eyes   160

---

141 Neoptolemus; *cf. n.*   mirable: *wonderful*
142 Oyes; *cf. n.*   145 expectance: *expectation*
147 issue: *result of the battle*   149 seld: *seldom*
154 signify: *make known*   155 *Cf. n.*

Shall find him by his large and portly size.

   Agam. Worthy of arms! as welcome as to one
That would be rid of such an enemy—
But that's no welcome.   Understand more clear,   164
What's past and what's to come is strew'd with husks
And formless ruin of oblivion;
But in this extant moment, faith and troth,
Strain'd purely from all hollow bias-drawing,   168
Bids thee, with most divine integrity,
From heart of very heart, great Hector, welcome.

   Hect. I thank thee, most imperious Agamemnon.

   Agam. [*To Troilus.*] My well-fam'd Lord of Troy,
    no less to you.   172

   Men. Let me confirm my princely brother's greeting.
You brace of warlike brothers, welcome hither.

   Hect. Who must we answer?

   Æne.   The noble Menelaus.

   Hect. O, you, my lord?   By Mars his gauntlet,
    thanks!   176
Mock not that I affect th' untraded oath;
Your *quondam* wife swears still by Venus' glove.
She's well, but bade me not commend her to you.

   Men. Name her not now, sir; she's a deadly
    theme.   180

   Hect. O, pardon!   I offend.

   Nest. I have, thou gallant Troyan, seen thee oft,
Labouring for destiny, make cruel way
Through ranks of Greekish youth, and I have seen
    thee,   184
As hot as Perseus, spur thy Phrygian steed,
And seen thee scorning forfeits and subduements,
When thou hast hung thy advanced sword i' th' air,

161 portly: *stately, imposing*   162, 163 as . . . enemy; *cf. n.*
168 *Cf. n.*   171 imperious: *imperial*
177 untraded: *unhackneyed*   183 Labouring for destiny; *cf. n.*
186 scorning . . . subduements; *cf. n.*   187 hung: *checked*

Not letting it decline on the declined,   188
That I have said unto my standers-by,
'Lo! Jupiter is yonder, dealing life!'
And I have seen thee pause and take thy breath,
When that a ring of Greeks have hemm'd thee in, 192
Like an Olympian wrestling.   This have I seen;
But this thy countenance, still lock'd in steel,
I never saw till now.   I knew thy grandsire,
And once fought with him.   He was a soldier good; 196
But, by great Mars, the captain of us all,
Never like thee.   Let an old man embrace thee;
And, worthy warrior, welcome to our tents.

 Æne. 'Tis the old Nestor.   200

 Hect. Let me embrace thee, good old chronicle,
That hast so long walk'd hand in hand with time.
Most reverend Nestor, I am glad to clasp thee.

 Nest. I would my arms could match thee in contention,   204
As they contend with thee in courtesy.

 Hect. I would they could.

 Nest. Ha!
By this white beard, I'd fight with thee to-morrow. 208
Well, welcome, welcome!   I have seen the time—

 Ulyss. I wonder now how yonder city stands,
When we have here her base and pillar by us.

 Hect. I know your favour, Lord Ulysses, well. 212
Ah, sir, there's many a Greek and Troyan dead,
Since first I saw yourself and Diomed
In Ilion, on your Greekish embassy.

 Ulyss. Sir, I foretold you then what would ensue. 216
My prophecy is but half his journey yet,
For yonder walls, that pertly front your town,
Yond towers, whose wanton tops do buss the clouds,

---

188 decline: *descend* declined: *fallen*
194 still: *ever*   219 buss: *kiss*

Must kiss their own feet.

　Hect.　　　　　　　I must not believe you. 220
There they stand yet, and modestly I think,
The fall of every Phrygian stone will cost
A drop of Grecian blood.　The end crowns all,
And that old common arbitrator, Time,　　　224
Will one day end it.

　Ulyss.　　　　So to him we leave it.
Most gentle and most valiant Hector, welcome.
After the general, I beseech you next
To feast with me and see me at my tent.　　228

　Achil. I shall forestall thee, Lord Ulysses, thou!
Now, Hector, I have fed mine eyes on thee;
I have with exact view perus'd thee, Hector,
And quoted joint by joint.

　Hect.　　　　　Is this Achilles?　　232

　Achil. I am Achilles.

　Hect. Stand fair, I prithee; let me look on thee.

　Achil. Behold thy fill.

　Hect.　　　　　Nay, I have done already.

　Achil. Thou art too brief.　I will the second time, 236
As I would buy thee, view thee limb by limb.

　Hect. O, like a book of sport thou'lt read me o'er;
But there's more in me than thou understand'st.
Why dost thou so oppress me with thine eye?　240

　Achil. Tell me, you heavens, in which part of his
　　body
Shall I destroy him, whether there, or there, or there?
That I may give the local wound a name,
And make distinct the very breach whereout　244
Hector's great spirit flew.　Answer me, heavens!

　Hect. It would discredit the bless'd gods, proud
　　man,

---

223 The end crowns all: *everything is judged by its result*
231 perus'd: *carefully examined*　　　　232 quoted: *noted*

To answer such a question.   Stand again.
Think'st thou to catch my life so pleasantly   248
As to prenominate in nice conjecture
Where thou wilt hit me dead?

   Achil.   I tell thee, yea.

   Hect. Wert thou the oracle to tell me so,
I'd not believe thee.   Henceforth guard thee well, 252
For I'll not kill thee there, nor there, nor there;
But, by the forge that stithied Mars his helm,
I'll kill thee everywhere, yea, o'er and o'er.
You wisest Grecians, pardon me this brag.   256
His insolence draws folly from my lips;
But I'll endeavour deeds to match these words,
Or may I never—

   Ajax.   Do not chafe thee, cousin;
And you, Achilles, let these threats alone,   260
Till accident or purpose bring you to 't.
You may have every day enough of Hector,
If you have stomach.   The general state, I fear,
Can scarce entreat you to be odd with him.   264

   Hect. I pray you, let us see you in the field.
We have had pelting wars since you refus'd
The Grecians' cause.

   Achil.   Dost thou entreat me, Hector?
To-morrow do I meet thee, fell as death;   268
To-night all friends.

   Hect.   Thy hand upon that match.

   Agam. First, all you peers of Greece, go to my tent;
There in the full convive you.   Afterwards,
As Hector's leisure and your bounties shall   272
Concur together, severally entreat him.

---

248 pleasantly: *flippantly*
249 prenominate: *foretell*   nice conjecture: *exact judgment*
254 stithied: *forged*   259 chafe: *anger*
261 to 't: *i.e. to an encounter*   263 state: *government*
264 odd: *at odds*   266 pelting: *paltry*   268 fell: *fierce*
271 convive: *feast together*   273 severally: *individually, separately*

Beat loud the tabourines, let the trumpets blow,
That this great soldier may his welcome know.

> *Exeunt* [*all except Troilus and Ulysses*].

Tro. My Lord Ulysses, tell me, I beseech you,   276
In what place of the field doth Calchas keep?

Ulyss. At Menelaus' tent, most princely Troilus.
There Diomed doth feast with him to-night;
Who neither looks on heaven nor on earth,   280
But gives all gaze and bent of amorous view
On the fair Cressid.

Tro. Shall I, sweet lord, be bound to thee so much,
After we part from Agamemnon's tent,   284
To bring me thither?

Ulyss.   You shall command me, sir.
As gentle tell me, of what honour was
This Cressida in Troy?   Had she no lover there
That wails her absence?   288

Tro. O, sir, to such as boasting show their scars
A mock is due.   Will you walk on, my lord?
She was belov'd, she lov'd; she is, and doth:
But still sweet love is food for fortune's tooth.   292

> *Exeunt.*

ACT FIFTH

Scene One

[*The Greek Camp.   Before Achilles' Tent*]

Enter Achilles and Patroclus.

Achil. I'll heat his blood with Greekish wine to-
     night,
Which with my scimitar I'll cool to-morrow.

---

274 tabourines: *drums*   277 keep: *dwell*
281 view: *looks*   286 gentle: *courteously*

Patroclus, let us feast him to the height.

Patr. Here comes Thersites.

Enter Thersites.

Achil.   How now, thou core of envy! 4
Thou crusty batch of nature, what's the news?

Ther. Why, thou picture of what thou
seem'st, and idol of idiot-worshippers, here's
a letter for thee.   8

Achil. From whence, fragment?

Ther. Why, thou full dish of fool, from Troy.

Patr. Who keeps the tent now?

Ther. The surgeon's box, or the patient's 12
wound.

Patr. Well said, adversity! and what need
these tricks?

Ther. Prithee, be silent, boy; I profit not 16
by thy talk. Thou art thought to be Achilles'
male varlet.

Patr. Male varlet, you rogue! What's that?

Ther. Why, his masculine whore. Now, the 20
rotten diseases of the south, guts-griping
ruptures, catarrhs, loads o' gravel i' th' back,
lethargies, cold palsies, [raw eyes, dirt-rotten
livers, wheezing lungs, bladders full of impos- 24
thume, sciaticas, lime-kilns i' the palm, incurable
bone-ache, and the rivelled fee-simple of the
tetter,] and the like, take and take again such
preposterous discoveries!   28

Patr. Why, thou damnable box of envy,

---

4 core: *centre, heart (particularly of a boil)*
5 batch: *amount of bread made at one baking*
12, 13 *Cf. n.*   24 imposthume: *pus, abscesses*
25 lime-kilns: *burning sensations* (?)
26 rivelled: *shrivelled*   fee-simple: *absolute ownership*
27 tetter: *a skin disease*   28 discoveries: *disclosures*

thou, what mean'st thou to curse thus?

Ther. Do I curse thee?

Patr. Why, no, you ruinous butt, you 32
whoreson indistinguishable cur, [no].

Ther. No? Why art thou then exasperate,
thou idle immaterial skein of sleave silk, thou
green sarcenet flap for a sore eye, thou tassel of 36
a prodigal's purse, thou? Ah, how the poor
world is pestered with such water-flies, diminutives of nature.

Patr. Out, gall!   40

Ther. Finch egg!

Achil. My sweet Patroclus, I am thwarted quite
From my great purpose in to-morrow's battle.
Here is a letter from Queen Hecuba,   44
A token from her daughter, my fair love,
Both taxing me and gaging me to keep
An oath that I have sworn. I will not break it.
Fall Greeks; fail fame; honour or go or stay; 48
My major vow lies here, this I'll obey.
Come, come, Thersites, help to trim my tent;
This night in banqueting must all be spent.
Away, Patroclus!   52

Exit [*with Patroclus*].

Ther. With too much blood and too little
brain, these two may run mad; but if with too
much brain, and too little blood they do, I'll be
a curer of madmen. Here's Agamemnon, an 56
honest fellow enough, and one that loves quails,
but he has not so much brain as ear-wax; and

---

32 butt: *cask*   33 indistinguishable: *of unrecognizable kind*
35 idle: *useless*   immaterial: *worthless*   sleave silk: *unspun silk,*
    floss; cf. n.   36 sarcenet: *silk*
38 diminutives: *small, mean objects*   42 thwarted: *turned aside*
46 gaging: *binding*   57 quails: *loose women*

the goodly transformation of Jupiter there, his
brother, the bull, the primitive statue, and 60
oblique memorial of cuckolds; a thrifty shoe-
ing-horn in a chain, hanging at his brother's
leg, to what form but that he is should wit
larded with malice and malice forced with wit 64
turn him to? To an ass, were nothing; he is both
ass and ox: to an ox, were nothing; he is both
ox and ass. To be a dog, a mule, a cat, a fitchew,
a toad, a lizard, an owl, a puttock, or a herring 68
without a roe, I would not care; but to be
Menelaus! I would conspire against destiny.
Ask me not what I would be, if I were not
Thersites, for I care not to be the louse of a 72
lazar, so I were not Menelaus. Hoy-day!
spirits and fires!

Enter Hector, Ajax, Agamemnon, Ulysses, Nestor,
Diomed, [Troilus, and Menelaus,] with lights.

Agam. We go wrong, we go wrong.
Ajax.   No, yonder 'tis;
There, where we see the lights.
Hect.   I trouble you.   76
Ajax. No, not a whit.
Ulyss.   Here comes himself to guide you.

Enter Achilles.

Achil. Welcome, brave Hector; welcome, princes all.
Agam. So now, fair prince of Troy, I bid good-
night.
Ajax commands the guard to tend on you.   80
Hect. Thanks and good-night to the Greeks' gen-
eral.

59-61 goodly . . . cuckolds; *cf. n.*
64 larded: *basted*
68 puttock: *kite*

61 oblique: *perverse*
67 fitchew: *polecat*
72 care . . . be: *should not mind being*

Men. Good-night, my lord.

Hect. Good-night, sweet Lord Menelaus.

   Ther. Sweet draught! 'Sweet,' quoth a'! Sweet 84
sink, sweet sewer.

Achil. Good-night and welcome both at once, to
   those
That go or tarry.

Agam. Good-night.   88
                    [*Exeunt Agamemnon and Menelaus.*]

Achil. Old Nestor tarries, and you too, Diomed,
Keep Hector company an hour or two.

Dio. I cannot, lord; I have important business,
The tide whereof is now. Good-night, great Hector. 92

Hect. Give me your hand.

Ulyss. [*Aside to Troilus.*] Follow his torch; he goes
   to Calchas' tent.
I'll keep you company.

Tro. Sweet sir, you honour me.

Hect.   And so, good-night. 96
                         [*Exit Diomedes; Ulysses and
                                  Troilus following.*]

Achil. Come, come, enter my tent.
      Exeunt [*Achilles, Hector, Ajax, and Nestor*].

   Ther. That same Diomed's a false-hearted
rogue, a most unjust knave; I will no more trust
him when he leers than I will a serpent when 100
he hisses. He will spend his mouth, and promise, like Brabbler the hound; but when he
performs, astronomers foretell it, that it is prodigious, there will come some change. The sun 104
borrows of the moon when Diomed keeps his
word. I will rather leave to see Hector, than

84 draught: *privy*   92 tide: *time*
101, 102 He . . . hound; *cf. n.*   103 prodigious: *portentous*
106 leave to see: *give up seeing*

not to dog him. They say he keeps a Troyan
drab, and uses the traitor Calchas' tent. I'll 108
after—nothing but lechery! All incontinent
varlets!   *Exit.*

Scene Two

[*The Same. Before Calchas' Tent*]

Enter Diomed.

Dio. What, are you up here, ho! Speak.
Cal. [*Within.*] Who calls?
Dio. Diomed. Calchas, I think. Where's your
     daughter?
Cal. [*Within.*] She comes to you.   4

Enter Troilus and Ulysses [*at a distance;
          after them Thersites*].

Ulyss. Stand where the torch may not discover us.

Enter Cressid.

Tro. Cressid comes forth to him.
Dio.   How now, my charge!
Cres. Now, my sweet guardian! Hark, a word with
     you.   [*Whispers.*]
Tro. Yea, so familiar!   8
Ulyss. She will sing any man at first sight.
     Ther. And any man may sing her, if he can
take her cliff; she's noted.
Dio. Will you remember?   12
Cres. Remember? Yes.
Dio. Nay, but do, then;
And let your mind be coupled with your words.
Tro. What should she remember?   16

10, 11 any . . . cliff; *cf. n.*   11 cliff: *clef, pitch*

Ulyss. List!

Cres. Sweet honey Greek, tempt me no more to folly.

Ther. Roguery!

Dio. Nay, then,—

Cres.   I'll tell you what,—   20

Dio. Foh, foh! come, tell a pin. You are a forsworn—

Cres. In faith, I cannot. What would you have me do?

Ther. A juggling trick,—to be secretly open.

Dio. What did you swear you would bestow on me?   24

Cres. I prithee, do not hold me to mine oath;
Bid me do anything but that, sweet Greek.

Dio. Good night.

Tro. Hold, patience!   28

Ulyss. How now, Troyan?

Cres. Diomed,—

Dio. No, no, good night; I'll be your fool no more.

Tro. Thy better must.

Cres.   Hark, one word in your ear. 32

Tro. O plague and madness!

Ulyss. You are mov'd, prince; let us depart, I pray you,
Lest your displeasure should enlarge itself
To wrathful terms. This place is dangerous;   36
The time right deadly. I beseech you, go.

Tro. Behold, I pray you!

Ulyss.   Nay, good my lord, go off;
You flow to great distraction; come, my lord.

Tro. I pray thee, stay.

Ulyss.   You have not patience; come. 40

---

21 tell a pin: *i.e. do not waste words; cf. n.*
39 flow: *are hastening*   distraction: *despair, madness*

Tro. I pray you, stay.   By hell, and all hell's tor-
   ments,
I will not speak a word!
   Dio.   And so, good night.
   Cres. Nay, but you part in anger.
   Tro.   Doth that grieve thee?
O wither'd truth!
   Ulyss.   Why, how now, lord!
   Tro.   By Jove, 44
I will be patient.
   Cres.   Guardian!   Why, Greek!
   Dio. Foh, foh! adieu; you palter.
   Cres. In faith, I do not.   Come hither once again.
   Ulyss. You shake, my lord, at something.   Will you
      go?   48
You will break out.
   Tro.   She strokes his cheek!
   Ulyss.   Come, come.
   Tro. Nay, stay; by Jove, I will not speak a word.
There is between my will and all offences
A guard of patience.   Stay a little while.   52
      Ther. How the devil Luxury, with his fat
   rump and potato finger, tickles these together!
   Fry, lechery, fry!
   Dio. But will you, then?   56
   Cres. In faith, I will, la; never trust me else.
   Dio. Give me some token for the surety of it.
   Cres. I'll fetch you one.   *Exit.*
   Ulyss. You have sworn patience.
   Tro.   Fear me not, sweet lord; 60
I will not be myself, nor have cognition
Of what I feel.   I am all patience.

---

41 all hell's; *cf. n.*   53 Luxury: *lechery*
54 potato finger; *cf. n.*   58 surety: *assurance*
61 cognition: *perception*

Enter Cressid.

Ther. Now the pledge; now, now, now!

Cres. Here, Diomed, keep this sleeve.   64

Tro. O beauty! where is thy faith?

Ulyss.   My lord,—

Tro. I will be patient; outwardly I will.

Cres. You look upon that sleeve; behold it well.

He lov'd me—O false wench! Give 't me again.   68

Dio. Whose was 't?

Cres.   It is no matter, now I have 't again.

I will not meet with you to-morrow night.

I prithee, Diomed, visit me no more.

Ther. Now she sharpens. Well said, whetstone!   72

Dio. I shall have it.

Cres.   What, this?

Dio.   Ay, that.

Cres. O, all you gods! O pretty, pretty pledge!

Thy master now lies thinking in his bed

Of thee and me, and sighs, and takes my glove,   76

And gives memorial dainty kisses to it,

As I kiss thee. Nay, do not snatch it from me;

He that takes that doth take my heart withal.

Dio. I had your heart before; this follows it.   80

Tro. I did swear patience.

Cres. You shall not have it, Diomed; faith, you
     shall not;

I'll give you something else.

Dio. I will have this. Whose was it?

Cres.   It is no matter. 84

Dio. Come, tell me whose it was.

Cres. 'Twas one's that lov'd me better than you will.

But, now you have it, take it.

   Dio.   Whose was it?

   Cres. By all Diana's waiting-women yond,   88
And by herself, I will not tell you whose.

   Dio. To-morrow will I wear it on my helm,
And grieve his spirit that dares not challenge it.

   Tro. Wert thou the devil, and wor'st it on thy
      horn,   92
It should be challeng'd.

   Cres. Well, well, 'tis done, 'tis past. And yet it is
      not;
I will not keep my word.

   Dio.   Why then, farewell;
Thou never shalt mock Diomed again.   96

   Cres. You shall not go. One cannot speak a word,
But it straight starts you.

   Dio.   I do not like this fooling.

   Ther. Nor I, by Pluto; but that that likes not me
Pleases me best.   100

   Dio. What, shall I come? The hour?

   Cres.   Ay, come,—O Jove!—
Do come.—I shall be plagu'd.

   Dio.   Farewell till then.

   Cres. Good night. I prithee, come.

                        Exit [*Diomedes*].

Troilus, farewell! One eye yet looks on thee,   104
But with my heart the other eye doth see.
Ah! poor our sex; this fault in us I find,
The error of our eye directs our mind.
What error leads must err. O, then conclude   108
Minds sway'd by eyes are full of turpitude.   *depravity*   *Exit.*

   Ther. A proof of strength she could not publish
      more,

---

88 Diana's waiting-women: *the stars*   98 starts: *excites*
99, 100 Nor I . . . best; *cf. n.*   102 plagu'd: *teased*
110 *Cf. n.*

Unless she say, 'My mind is now turn'd whore.'

   Ulyss. All's done, my lord.

   Tro.   It is.

   Ulyss.   Why stay we, then? 112

   Tro. To make a recordation to my soul

Of every syllable that here was spoke.

But if I tell how these two did co-act,

Shall I not lie in publishing a truth?   116

Sith yet there is a credence in my heart,

An esperance so obstinately strong,

That doth invert th' attest of eyes and ears,

As if those organs had deceptious functions,   120

Created only to calumniate.

Was Cressid here?

   Ulyss.   I cannot conjure, Troyan.

   Tro. She was not, sure.

   Ulyss.   Most sure she was.

   Tro. Why, my negation hath no taste of madness. 124

   Ulyss. Nor mine, my lord. Cressid was here but
now.

   Tro. Let it not be believ'd for womanhood!

Think we had mothers; do not give advantage

To stubborn critics, apt, without a theme,   128

For depravation, to square the general sex

By Cressid's rule. Rather think this not Cressid.

   Ulyss. What hath she done, prince, that can soil
our mothers?

   Tro. Nothing at all, unless that this were she. 132

   Ther. Will he swagger himself out on 's own eyes?

   Tro. This she? No, this is Diomed's Cressida.

If beauty have a soul, this is not she;

---

113 recordation: *note, record*   118 esperance: *hope*
119 attest: *testimony; cf. n.*   120 deceptious: *delusive*
122 conjure: *raise spirits*   124 taste: *suggestion*
126 for: *for the sake of*   127 advantage: *assistance*
129 depravation: *slander*   square: *measure*   general sex: *sex in*
     general   133 on: *of the evidence of*

If souls guide vows, if vows are sanctimony,   136
If sanctimony be the gods' delight,
If there be rule in unity itself,
This is not she.   O madness of discourse,
That cause sets up with and against itself;   140
Bi-fold authority, where reason can revolt
Without perdition, and loss assume all reason
Without revolt.   This is, and is not, Cressid.
Within my soul there doth conduce a fight   144
Of this strange nature that a thing inseparate
Divides more wider than the sky and earth;
And yet the spacious breadth of this division
Admits no orifice for a point as subtle   148
As Ariachne's broken woof to enter.
Instance, O instance! strong as Pluto's gates;
Cressid is mine, tied with the bonds of heaven.
Instance, O instance! strong as heaven itself;   152
The bonds of heaven are slipp'd, dissolv'd, and loos'd;
And with another knot, five-finger-tied,
The fractions of her faith, orts of her love,
The fragments, scraps, the bits, and greasy relics 156
Of her o'er-eaten faith, are bound to Diomed.
    Ulyss. May worthy Troilus be half attach'd
With that which here his passion doth express?
    Tro. Ay, Greek; and that shall be divulged well 160
In characters as red as Mars his heart
Inflam'd with Venus.   Never did young man fancy
With so eternal and so fix'd a soul.
Hark, Greek: as much [as] I do Cressid love,   164
So much by weight hate I her Diomed;

136 sanctimony: *something sacred*   138 *Cf. n.*
139-143 O . . . revolt; *cf. n.*   141 Bi-fold; *cf. n.*
144 conduce: *go on*   145 inseparate: *inseparable*
148 subtle: *fine*   149 Ariachne's; *cf. n.*
150 Instance: *evidence*
154 five-finger-tied: *tied very securely* (?)
155 orts: *fragments*   158, 159 *Cf. n.*   164 much as I; *cf. n.*

That sleeve is mine that he'll bear in his helm;
Were it a casque compos'd by Vulcan's skill,
My sword should bite it.   Not the dreadful spout   168
Which shipmen do the hurricano call,
Constring'd in mass by the almighty sun,
Shall dizzy with more clamour Neptune's ear
In his descent than shall my prompted sword   172
Falling on Diomed.
    Ther. He'll tickle it for his concupy.
    Tro. O Cressid! O false Cressid! false, false, false!
Let all untruths stand by thy stained name,   176
And they'll seem glorious.
    Ulyss.   O! contain yourself;
Your passion draws ears hither.

Enter Æneas.

    Æne. I have been seeking you this hour, my lord.
Hector, by this, is arming him in Troy;   180
Ajax, your guard, stays to conduct you home.
    Tro. Have with you, prince.   My courteous lord,
    adieu.
Farewell, revolted fair! and Diomed,
Stand fast, and wear a castle on thy head!   184
    Ulyss. I'll bring you to the gates.
    Tro. Accept distracted thanks.

Exeunt Troilus, Æneas, and Ulysses.

    Ther. Would I could meet that rogue Dio-
med!   I would croak like a raven; I would bode, 188
I would bode.   Patroclus will give me anything for the intelligence of this whore.   The

169 hurricano: *waterspout*
170 Constring'd: *drawn together*   sun; *cf. n.*
172 prompted: *ready*
174 it: *him* (Diomed)   concupy: *concubine*
182 Have with you: *come on*
183 revolted: *i.e. faithless*   fair: *beauty*
184 castle: *the strongest possible protection*
188 bode: *forebode, be ominous*
190 intelligence: *knowledge, information*

parrot will not do more for an almond than
he for a commodious drab. Lechery, lechery; 192
still wars and lechery; nothing else holds
fashion. A burning devil take them!   [*Exit.*]

Scene Three

[*Troy. Before Priam's Palace*]

Enter Hector and Andromache.

And. When was my lord so much ungently temper'd,
To stop his ears against admonishment?
Unarm, unarm, and do not fight to-day.

Hect. You train me to offend you; get you gone.   4
By all the everlasting gods, I'll go.

And. My dreams will, sure, prove ominous to the
   day.

Hect. No more, I say.

Enter Cassandra.

Cas.   Where is my brother Hector?
And. Here, sister; arm'd, and bloody in intent.   8
Consort with me in loud and dear petition;
Pursue we him on knees, for I have dream'd
Of bloody turbulence, and this whole night
Hath nothing been but shapes and forms of slaugh-
   ter.   12

Cas. O, 'tis true.
Hect.   Ho! bid my trumpet sound.
Cas. No notes of sally, for the heavens, sweet
   brother.
Hect. Be gone, I say; the gods have heard me swear.

191 parrot . . . almond; *cf. n.*   4 train: *tempt, lead on*
6 ominous . . . day; *cf. n.*   9 Consort: *join*   dear: *earnest*

   Cas. The gods are deaf to hot and peevish vows. 16
They are polluted offerings, more abhorr'd
Than spotted livers in the sacrifice.
   And. O, be persuaded! Do not count it holy
To hurt by being just. It is as lawful,   20
For we would give much, to use violent thefts,
And rob in the behalf of charity.
   Cas. It is the purpose that makes strong the vow;
But vows to every purpose must not hold.   24
Unarm, sweet Hector.
   Hect.   Hold you still, I say;
Mine honour keeps the weather of my fate.
Life every man holds dear; but the dear man
Holds honour far more precious-dear than life. 28

Enter Troilus.

How now, young man! Mean'st thou to fight to-day?
   And. Cassandra, call my father to persuade.
                    Exit Cassandra.
   Hect. No, faith, young Troilus; doff thy harness,
     youth;
I am to-day i' th' vein of chivalry.   32
Let grow thy sinews till their knots be strong,
And tempt not yet the brushes of the war.
Unarm thee, go, and doubt thou not, brave boy,
I'll stand to-day for thee and me and Troy.   36
   Tro. Brother, you have a vice of mercy in you,
Which better fits a lion than a man.
   Hect. What vice is that, good Troilus? Chide me
     for it.
   Tro. When many times the captive Grecian falls, 40
Even in the fan and wind of your fair sword,

---

16 peevish: *foolish*   21 *Cf. n.*
25 Hold you still: *keep silent*   26 keeps . . . fate; *cf. n.*
31 harness: *armor*   34 brushes: *encounters*
38 lion; *cf. n.*

You bid them rise, and live.

 Hect. O, 'tis fair play.

 Tro.   Fool's play, by heaven, Hector.

 Hect. How now! how now!

 Tro.   For th' love of all the gods, 44
Let's leave the hermit pity with our mothers,
And when we have our armours buckled on,
The venom'd vengeance ride upon our swords,
Spur them to ruthful work, rein them from ruth.   48

 Hect. Fie, savage, fie!

 Tro.   Hector, then 'tis wars.

 Hect. Troilus, I would not have you fight to-day.

 Tro. Who should withhold me?
Not fate, obedience, nor the hand of Mars   52
Beck'ning with fiery truncheon my retire;
Not Priamus and Hecuba on knees,
Their eyes o'ergalled with recourse of tears;
Nor you, my brother, with your true sword drawn, 56
Oppos'd to hinder me, should stop my way,
But by my ruin.

Enter Priam and Cassandra.

 Cas. Lay hold upon him, Priam, hold him fast;
He is thy crutch. Now if thou lose thy stay,   60
Thou on him leaning, and all Troy on thee,
Fall all together.

 Pri.   Come, Hector, come; go back.
Thy wife hath dream'd; thy mother hath had visions;
Cassandra doth foresee; and I myself   64
Am like a prophet suddenly enrapt,
To tell thee that this day is ominous:
Therefore, come back.

48 ruthful: *piteous* ruth: *pity*
53 truncheon: *staff of authority* retire: *retreat*
55 o'ergalled: *irritated* recourse: *frequent flowing*
65 enrapt: *seized with prophetic frenzy*

Hect.   Æneas is a-field;
And I do stand engag'd to many Greeks,   68
Even in the faith of valour, to appear
This morning to them.
    Pri.   Ay, but thou shalt not go.
    Hect. I must not break my faith.
You know me dutiful; therefore, dear sir,   72
Let me not shame respect, but give me leave
To take that course by your consent and voice,
Which you do here forbid me, royal Priam.
    Cas. O Priam, yield not to him!
    And.   Do not, dear father. 76
    Hect. Andromache, I am offended with you.
Upon the love you bear me, get you in.
                                        Exit Andromache.
    Tro. This foolish, dreaming, superstitious girl
Makes all these bodements.
    Cas.   O farewell, dear Hector! 80
Look, how thou diest; look, how thy eye turns pale;
Look, how thy wounds doth bleed at many vents!
Hark, how Troy roars; how Hecuba cries out!
How poor Andromache shrills her dolour forth!   84
Behold, distraction, frenzy, and amazement,
Like witless antics, one another meet,
And all cry Hector! Hector's dead! O Hector!
    Tro. Away! Away!   88
    Cas. Farewell. Yet, soft! Hector, I take my leave.
Thou dost thyself and all our Troy deceive.   *Exit.*
    Hect. You are amaz'd, my liege, at her exclaim.
Go in and cheer the town. We'll forth and fight;   92
Do deeds worth praise and tell you them at night.

69 in . . . valour; *cf. n.*   73 respect: *filial duty*
74 voice: *agreement*   80 bodements: *forebodings*
86 antics: *buffoons, idiots*   91 exclaim: *outcry*

Pri. Farewell! The gods with safety stand about
   thee!

   [*Exeunt severally Priam and Hector.*]   *Alarum.*
Tro. They are at it, hark! Proud Diomed, believe,
I come to lose my arm, or win my sleeve.   96

   Enter Pandar [*as Troilus is going out*].

Pan. Do you hear, my lord? Do you hear?
Tro. What now?
Pan. Here's a letter come from yond poor girl.
Tro. Let me read.   100
   Pan. A whoreson tisick, a whoreson rascally
tisick so troubles me, and the foolish fortune of
this girl; and what one thing, what another,
that I shall leave you one o' these days; and I   104
have a rheum in mine eyes too, and such an
ache in my bones that, unless a man were
cursed, I cannot tell what to think on 't. What
says she there?   108
Tro. Words, words, mere words, no matter from the
   heart;
Th' effect doth operate another way.

                        [*Tearing the letter.*]
Go, wind to wind, there turn and change together.
My love with words and errors still she feeds,   112
But edifies another with her deeds.
   Pan. Why, but hear you!
   Tro. Hence, brother lackey! Ignomy and shame
Pursue thy life and live aye with thy name!   116
                                    Exeunt.

101 tisick: *cough*   110 *Cf. n.*
114-116 *Cf. n.*   115 Ignomy: *ignominy*

Scene Four

[Between Troy and the Greek Camp]

Alarum. Enter Thersites in excursion.

Ther. Now they are clapper-clawing one another; I'll go look on. That dissembling abominable varlet, Diomed, has got that same scurvy doting foolish young knave's sleeve of Troy there 4 in his helm. I would fain see them meet, that that same young Troyan ass, that loves the whore there, might send that Greekish whoremasterly villain, with the sleeve, back to the dissembling 8 luxurious drab, of a sleeveless errand. O' th' tother side, the policy of those crafty swearing rascals,—that stale old mouse-eaten dry cheese, Nestor, and that same dog-fox, Ulysses, is not 12 prov'd worth a blackberry. They set me up, in policy, that mongrel cur, Ajax, against that dog of as bad a kind, Achilles. And now is the cur Ajax prouder than the cur Achilles, and will 16 not arm to-day. Whereupon the Grecians begin to proclaim barbarism, and policy grows into an ill opinion. *Enter Diomed and Troilus.* Soft! here comes sleeve, and th' other. 20

Tro. Fly not; for shouldst thou take the river Styx, I would swim after.

Dio.   Thou dost miscall retire.
I do not fly, but advantageous care
Withdrew me from the odds of multitude. 24
Have at thee!

Scene Four S. d. in excursion: *running on*
1 clapper-clawing: *mauling*
9 luxurious: *lustful*   sleeveless: *bootless (with a quibble)*
13 set me up; *cf. n.*   18 to proclaim barbarism; *cf. n.*
23, 24 advantageous . . . multitude; *cf. n.*

Ther. Hold thy whore, Grecian! Now for thy
whore, Troyan! Now the sleeve, now the sleeve!
> [*Exeunt Troilus and Diomedes, fighting.*]

Enter Hector.

Hect. What art thou, Greek? Art thou for Hector's
match?   28
Art thou of blood and honour?

Ther. No, no, I am a rascal; a scurvy railing
knave; a very filthy rogue.

Hect. I do believe thee; live.   [*Exit.*] 32

Ther. God-a-mercy, that thou wilt believe
me; but a plague break thy neck—for frighting
me! What's become of the wenching rogues?
I think they have swallowed one another. I 36
would laugh at that miracle;—yet, in a sort,
lechery eats itself. I'll seek them.   *Exit.*

Scene Five

[Another Part of the Plains]

Enter Diomed and Servants.

Dio. Go, go, my servant, take thou Troilus' horse;
Present the fair steed to my Lady Cressid.
Fellow, commend my service to her beauty;
Tell her I have chastis'd the amorous Troyan,   4
And am her knight by proof.

Serv.   I go, my lord. [*Exit.*]

Enter Agamemnon.

Agam. Renew, renew! The fierce Polydamas
Hath beat down Menon; bastard Margarelon
Hath Doreus prisoner,   8

---

33 God-a-mercy: *thanks*   7 Margarelon: *a bastard son of Priam*

And stands colossus-wise, waving his beam,
Upon the pashed corses of the kings
Epistrophus and Cedius; Polyxenes is slain;
Amphimachus, and Thoas, deadly hurt;   12
Patroclus ta'en, or slain; and Palamedes
Sore hurt and bruis'd.   The dreadful Sagittary
Appals our numbers.   Haste we, Diomed,
To reinforcement, or we perish all.   16

Enter Nestor.

Nest. Go, bear Patroclus' body to Achilles;
And bid the snail-pac'd Ajax arm for shame.
There is a thousand Hectors in the field.
Now here he fights on Galathe his horse,   20
And there lacks work; anon he's there afoot,
And there they fly or die, like scaled sculls
Before the belching whale; then is he yonder,
And there the straying Greeks, ripe for his edge,   24
Fall down before him, like the mower's swath.
Here, there, and everywhere, he leaves and takes,
Dexterity so obeying appetite
That what he will he does, and does so much   28
That proof is call'd impossibility.

Enter Ulysses.

Ulyss. O, courage, courage, princes! Great Achilles
Is arming, weeping, cursing, vowing vengeance.
Patroclus' wounds have rous'd his drowsy blood,   32
Together with his mangled Myrmidons,
That noseless, handless, hack'd and chipp'd, come to
    him,
Crying on Hector.   Ajax hath lost a friend,

9 beam: *lance*   14 Sagittary; *cf. n.*
22 sculls: *schools (of fish)*   23 belching: *spouting*
24 edge: *sword*   27 appetite: *desire*
29 proof: *thing proved, fact*   35 on: *out against*

And foams at mouth, and he is arm'd and at it,   36
Roaring for Troilus, who hath done to-day
Mad and fantastic execution,
Engaging and redeeming of himself
With such a careless force and forceless care   40
As if that luck, in very spite of cunning,
Bade him win all.

Enter Ajax.

Ajax. Troilus! thou coward Troilus!   *Exit.*
Dio.   Ay, there, there.
Nest. So, so, we draw together.

Enter Achilles.

Achil.   Where is this Hector? 44
Come, come, thou boy-queller, show thy face;
Know what it is to meet Achilles angry.
Hector! where's Hector? I will none but Hector.
                        Exeunt.

Scene Six

[*Another Part of the Plains*]

Enter Ajax.

Ajax. Troilus, thou coward Troilus, show thy head!

Enter Diomed.

Dio. Troilus, I say! where's Troilus?
Ajax.   What wouldst thou?
Dio. I would correct him.
Ajax. Were I the general, thou shouldst have my
    office   4
Ere that correction. Troilus, I say! what, Troilus!

38 fantastic: *prodigious*   40 forceless care: *easy skill*
41 spite: *scorn*   45 queller: *killer*

Enter Troilus.

Tro. O traitor Diomed! Turn thy false face, thou traitor,

And pay thy life thou owest me for my horse!

Dio. Ha, art thou there?   8

Ajax. I'll fight with him alone. Stand, Diomed.

Dio. He is my prize; I will not look upon.

Tro. Come, both you cogging Greeks; have at you both!   [*Exeunt, fighting.*]

Enter Hector.

Hect. Yea, Troilus? O, well fought, my youngest brother!   12

Enter Achilles.

Achil. Now do I see thee. Have at thee, Hector!

Hect. Pause, if thou wilt.

Achil. I do disdain thy courtesy, proud Troyan.

Be happy that my arms are out of use.   16

My rest and negligence befriends thee now,

But thou anon shalt hear of me again;

Till when, go seek thy fortune.   *Exit.*

Hect.   Fare thee well:

I would have been much more a fresher man,   20

Had I expected thee. How now, my brother!

Enter Troilus.

Tro. Ajax hath ta'en Æneas! Shall it be?

No, by the flame of yonder glorious heaven,

He shall not carry him; I'll be ta'en too,   24

Or bring him off. Fate, hear me what I say!

I reck not though thou end my life to-day.   *Exit.*

Enter one in [sumptuous] armour.

10 upon: *on*
16 use: *practice*   24 carry: *retain*   11 cogging: *cheating*
26 reck: *care*

Hect. Stand, stand, thou Greek; thou art a goodly
      mark.
No? Wilt thou not? I like thy armour well;   28
I'll frush it, and unlock the rivets all,
But I'll be master of it. Wilt thou not, beast, abide?
Why then, fly on, I'll hunt thee for thy hide.

                                             Exeunt.

                        Scene Seven

                [Another Part of the Plains]

                Enter Achilles, with Myrmidons.

Achil. Come here about me, you my Myrmidons;
Mark what I say. Attend me where I wheel;
Strike not a stroke, but keep yourselves in breath;
And when I have the bloody Hector found,   4
Empale him with your weapons round about;
In fellest manner execute your arms.
Follow me, sirs, and my proceedings eye.
It is decreed, Hector the great must die.   8

                            Exit [with Myrmidons].

          *Enter Thersites, [then] Menelaus and
                     Paris [fighting].*

Ther. The cuckold and the cuckold-maker
are at it. Now, bull! now, dog! 'Loo, Paris,
'loo! Now, my double-henn'd sparrow! 'Loo,
Paris, 'loo! The bull has the game; 'ware 12
horns, ho!   *Exeunt Paris and Menelaus.*

              Enter Bastard [Margarelon].

Bast. Turn, slave, and fight.

29 frush: *batter*   5 Empale: *enclose*
6 execute: *make use of; cf. n.*   10 'Loo: *halloo*
11 double-henn'd sparrow; *cf. n.*

Ther. What art thou?

Bast. A bastard son of Priam's.   16

Ther. I am a bastard too; I love bastards. I
am a bastard begot, bastard instructed, bastard
in mind, bastard in valour, in everything illegi-
timate. One bear will not bite another, and 20
wherefore should one bastard? Take heed, the
quarrel's most ominous to us. If the son of a
whore fight for a whore, he tempts judgment.
Farewell, bastard.   24

Bast. The devil take thee, coward!   *Exeunt.*

Scene Eight

[Another Part of the Plains]

Enter Hector.

Hect. Most putrefied core, so fair without,
Thy goodly armour thus hath cost thy life.
Now is my day's work done; I'll take good breath.
Rest, sword; thou hast thy fill of blood and death.   4
     *[Puts off his helmet, and hangs
          his shield behind him.]*

Enter Achilles and his Myrmidons.

Achil. Look, Hector, how the sun begins to set;
How ugly night comes breathing at his heels.
Even with the vail and darking of the sun,
To close the day up, Hector's life is done.   8

Hect. I am unarm'd; forgo this vantage, Greek.

Achil. Strike, fellows, strike; this is the man I seek.
     [Hector falls.]

So, Ilion, fall thou [next]! Now, Troy, sink down!
Here lies thy heart, thy sinews, and thy bone.   12

---

7 vail: *sinking*

On! Myrmidons, [and] cry you all amain,
'Achilles hath the mighty Hector slain!'

Retreat.

Hark! a retreat upon our Grecian part.
  Greek. The Troyan trumpets sound the like, my
    lord.   16
  Achil. The dragon wing of night o'erspreads the
    earth,
And, stickler-like, the armies separates.
My half-supp'd sword, that frankly would have fed,
Pleas'd with this dainty bait, thus goes to bed.   20
                            [Sheathes his sword.]
Come, tie his body to my horse's tail;
Along the field I will the Troyan trail.   *Exeunt.*

Scene Nine

[Another Part of the Plains]

*Enter Agamemnon, Ajax, Menelaus, Nestor, Diomed,
and the rest, marching.*

Sound retreat. Shout.

  Agam. Hark! hark! what shout is that?
  Nest.   Peace, drums!
  Sold[*iers within.*]   Achilles!
Achilles! Hector's slain! Achilles!
  Dio. The bruit is, Hector's slain, and by Achilles.
  Ajax. If it be so, yet bragless let it be;   4
Great Hector was a man as good as he.
  Agam. March patiently along. Let one be sent
To pray Achilles see us at our tent.

13 amain: *vehemently*   18 stickler-like; *cf. n.*
19 frankly: *freely*   20 bait: *food, meal; cf. n.*
3 bruit: *rumor*

If in his death the gods have us befriended,   8
Great Troy is ours, and our sharp wars are ended.

Exeunt.

Scene Ten

[Another Part of the Plains]

Enter Æneas, Paris, Antenor, and Deiphobus.

Æne. Stand, ho! yet are we masters of the field.
Never go home; here starve we out the night.

Enter Troilus.

Tro. Hector is slain.
All.   Hector! The gods forbid!
Tro. He's dead; and at the murtherer's horse's
     tail,   4
In beastly sort, dragg'd through the shameful field.
Frown on, you heavens, effect your rage with speed!
Sit, gods, upon your thrones, and smile at Troy!
I say, at once let your brief plagues be mercy,   8
And linger not our sure destructions on!
Æne. My lord, you do discomfort all the host.
Tro. You understand me not that tell me so.
I do not speak of flight, of fear, of death,   12
But dare all imminence that gods and men
Address their dangers in.   Hector is gone.
Who shall tell Priam so, or Hecuba?
Let him that will a screech-owl aye be call'd   16
Go in to Troy, and say there Hector's dead.
There is a word will Priam turn to stone,
Make wells and Niobes of the maids and wives,
Cold statues of the youth; and, in a word,   20
Scare Troy out of itself.   But march away.

10 discomfort: *dishearten*   13, 14 But . . . in; *cf. n.*

Hector is dead; there is no more to say.
Stay yet. You vile abominable tents,
Thus proudly pight upon our Phrygian plains,   24
Let Titan rise as early as he dare,
I'll through and through you! And, thou great-siz'd
          coward,
No space of earth shall sunder our two hates.
I'll haunt thee like a wicked conscience still,   28
That mouldeth goblins swift as frenzy's thoughts.
Strike a free march to Troy! With comfort go;
Hope of revenge shall hide our inward woe.

                    [*Exeunt Æneas and Trojan Forces.*]

          Enter Pandarus [*as Troilus is going out*].

Pan. But hear you, hear you!   32
     Tro. Hence, broker lackey! Ignomy and shame
Pursue thy life, and live aye with thy name!   *Exit.*
     Pan. A goodly med'cine for mine aching bones!
O world! world! world! thus is the poor agent 36
despised. O traitors and bawds, how earnestly
are you set a-work, and how ill requited! Why
should our endeavour be so desired, and the performance so loathed? What verse for it? What 40
instance for it?—Let me see!—
     'Full merrily the humble-bee doth sing,
          Till he hath lost his honey and his sting;
          And being once subdu'd in armed tail,   44
          Sweet honey and sweet notes together fail.'
Good traders in the flesh, set this in your
painted cloths:
'As many as be here of Pandar's hall,   48
     Your eyes, half out, weep out at Pandar's fall;

24 pight: *pitched*   25 Titan: *the sun*
33 broker: *go-between*
47 painted cloths: *hangings for walls*

Or if you cannot weep, yet give some groans,
Though not for me, yet for your aching bones.
Brethren and sisters of the hold-door trade,   52
Some two months hence my will shall here be made.
It should be now, but that my fear is this,
Some galled goose of Winchester would hiss.
Till then I'll sweat, and seek about for eases;   56
And at that time bequeath you my diseases.'   *Exit.*

52 Brethren . . . trade: *pimps and bawds*
55 galled goose of Winchester; *cf. n.*   56 sweat; *cf. n.*

FINIS.

NOTES

A Never Writer to an Ever Reader. News. This curious epistle, clearly written for advertising purposes, was prefixed to the second issue of the Quarto of 1609, and raises the question of the early history of the play. (See Appendix B.) It is not improbable that the play was never presented on the stage, and that this curious fact was not discovered by the publishers until a part of the edition, with the original title-page, had been issued. If this was the case, they were, of course, quick to capitalize such an unusual situation and to take advantage of the popular interest in Shakespeare. The 'grand possessors' would then be, not the actors, as has been generally supposed, but the friends of the company who owned manuscript copies of the play, from one of which the Quarto seems to have been printed. The uncertain structure of the end of the play seems to support this view. If, on the other hand, the play actually was acted by 'the King's Majesty's Servants at the Globe,' as is stated on the first title-page, two possibilities remain. Either the publishers disregarded the truth for mercenary reasons, or the play, as they printed it, had been altered from the acting version by additions or omissions, so that it was technically a different play. With the present lack of definite knowledge of the early history of the play a final explanation of the epistle is impossible.

The Prologue. The Prologue, which does not appear in the Quarto, has been generally attributed to another hand than Shakespeare's on alleged considerations of style. Chapman has been suggested as a possible author, but there is not sufficient evidence for denying its genuineness.

Prol. 17. *Antenonidus.* This name is usually changed to *Antenorides,* the form in which it appears in Caxton. In Lydgate the gate is called *Anthonydes.*

Prol. 19. *Sperr.* The Folio reading is *stir.* Theobald's emendation here given is generally accepted. Chaucer uses *sperred,* closed, of doors in *Troilus and Criseyde.*

Prol. 23-25. *A prologue arm'd . . . argument.* The Prologue ordinarily wore a black cloak. Here his armor is meant to fit the subject of the warlike play, not to express the defiance of either author or actors as the 'armed Prologue' in Ben Jonson's *Poetaster* (1601) had done.

Act First. The division into acts and scenes is found in neither Folio nor Quarto except for the heading *Actus Primus: Scœna Prima* in the Folio. It was first made by Rowe (ed. 1709).

I. i. 33. *So, traitor, then she comes, when she is thence.* Troilus, breaking off his original train of thought, calls himself a traitor for admitting that Cressida is ever absent from his thoughts and says that when she is absent for a moment she instantly returns. This is the reading of the Folio and Quarto. Rowe, followed by many modern editors, 'corrects' the line to, 'So, traitor!—"When she comes!"—When is she thence?'

I. i. 39. *a storm.* The reading of the Folio is *a-scorn,* that of the Quarto, *a scorn.* This emendation, by Rowe, is generally adopted by modern editors.

I. i. 60. *spirit of sense.* Various emendations have been proposed for this somewhat obscure line. The words probably refer to 'the most exquisite power of sensibility.' (Johnson.)

I. i. 80, 81. *as fair on Friday as Helen is on Sunday.* 'She would be as fair in her plainest dress as Helen in her most gorgeous finery.' Clarke suggests the added idea of Friday as a day of abstinence and Sunday as a day of festival.

I. i. 85. *She's a fool to stay behind her father.* Calchas, according to Caxton, was 'a great learned bishop of Troy.' He was sent by Priam to consult the oracle of Delphi concerning the outcome of the war threatened by Agamemnon. Apollo told him that the Greeks were to be victorious by agreement of the gods, and urged him to desert to their army. This Calchas did, leaving Cressida in Troy.

I. i. 97. *I cannot fight upon this argument.* A quibble on the ideas of fighting for such a cause and of fighting on an empty stomach.

I. i. 103. *Daphne's.* Daphne was the nymph who was changed into a laurel tree when she fled from Apollo.

I. i. 117. *Menelaus' horn.* The usual allusion to the horns which were supposed to grow on the foreheads of deceived husbands.

I. ii. 5. *Is as a virtue fix'd.* 'Is of the nature of a fixed and stable virtue.'

I. ii. 23. *humours.* The four real or imaginary fluids in the body, according to the physiology of Shakespeare's time, which were believed to determine temperament and, when not in proper proportion, to produce disease. Peculiarities of manner, thought to be attributable to these fluids, were called *humors*.

I. ii. 23, 24. *his valour is crush'd into folly, his folly sauced with discretion.* 'Valor and folly are so crushed together, and folly is so seasoned with discretion that it is difficult to tell one quality from another in him.'

I. ii. 30. *Briareus.* A mythical giant with a hundred hands.

I. ii. 31. *Argus.* A mythical giant with a hundred eyes.

I. ii. 44. *cousin.* This word was loosely used to indicate collateral relationship of any kind.

I. ii. 46. *Ilium.* Priam's palace, according to Caxton, was named *Ilium* or *Ilion.*

I. ii. 78. *Condition, I had gone bare-foot to India.* 'I would he were, even though I had had to go barefoot to India to make him so.'

I. ii. 90. *will.* This is the reading of both Folio and Quarto. Most modern editors follow Rowe's emendation to *wit.*

I. ii. 116. *merry Greek.* A play upon the familiar name for a roisterer or reveller. Mathewe Merygreeke is such a character in Udall's *Ralph Roister Doister* (c. 1553).

I. ii. 156. *With millstones.* A proverbial and mocking way of saying that Hecuba wept no tears at all.

I. ii. 169. *two-and-fifty.* Theobald, followed by many modern editors, altered this to *one-and-fifty,* since Priam traditionally had fifty sons. Possibly the bastard Margarelon who appears later (V. v. 7), makes the fifty-first, although this point is disputed.

I. ii. 211. *the rich shall have more.* There is a pun here, referring to the word *nod* in l. 208, on *nod* or *noddy,* meaning *a simpleton.* The allusion is to the Biblical sentence, 'To him that hath shall be given'; a nod shall be given to him who is already noddy.

I. ii. 221. *there's laying on.* 'The hacks on his helmet are proof of the fierceness of the fight.'

I. ii. 262. *i' th' eyes of Troilus.* 'Looking at Troilus,' or, perhaps, 'with Troilus looking at me.'

I. ii. 278. *date.* Dates were often used as seasoning in pies, and were supposed to rouse sexual desire. There is also, of course, a pun on the word *date* in the sense of *allotted time.*

I. ii. 281. *at what ward you lie.* 'What your pos-

ture of defense is.' A term in fencing. He means,
'I do not know how to take you.'

I. ii. 287. *watches.* Here, and in the following
two speeches the speakers are quibbling on the word
in its double meaning of *being vigilant* and *staying
awake at night.*

I. ii. 303. *To bring.* A slang expression which
often appears. Its meaning is uncertain, but seems to
be, 'I'll get even with you.'

I. ii. 317. *Achievement is command; ungain'd, beseech.* 'When men have achieved what they desire
they become masters and command; while they are
being held in suspense they are content to beseech.'

I. iii. 8. *diverts.* The third person plural of the
present indicative of verbs frequently ends in s in
Shakespeare: cf. *tends* (II. iii. 136), *speaks* (III. ii.
159), *Wants* (III. ii. 183), *meets* (IV. i. 16).

I. iii. 13-17. *Sith . . . shape.* This passage is so
compressed that its syntax is not clear. It means,
'since trial has drawn awry and crosswise every previous action of which we have record, so that it has
not corresponded to the aim of its originator nor to
the impalpable shape which it assumed in thought.'
Bias is a technical term in bowling, referring to the
weight placed on one side of the bowl to make it roll
a peculiar way.

I. iii. 39. *Thetis.* A sea goddess, the mother of
Achilles, here, as often, confounded with Tethys, the
wife of Oceanus, and used as the personification of
the sea.

I. iii. 41. *moist elements.* 'In the old "natural
philosophy" air and water were called the moist elements, earth and fire the dry.' (Tatlock.)

I. iii. 42. *Perseus' horse.* Pegasus, who sprang
from the blood of Medusa, actually belonged to
Bellerophon. According to Ovid, however, Perseus
rode him when he went to rescue Andromeda from the

sea monster, and he is frequently referred to as Perseus' horse by Elizabethan writers.

I. iii. 54. *Retorts*. This word is emended, by Dyce, from the *Retires* of both Folio and Quarto. Among other proposed emendations are *Re-chides* (Lettsom), *Returns* (Pope), and *Replies* (Hanmer).

I. iii. 62-68. *which . . . tongue*. This difficult passage, which may be corrupt, has been variously emended. Its sense seems to be, '(speeches) which were such as, in the case of Agamemnon's, should be engraved in brass and held up by Agamemnon and Greece together to show the unanimity of their ideas, and, in the case of Nestor's, should unite all the Greeks by the bond of his voice which, though impalpable, should be as strong as the axletree on which the heavens ride.' *Hatch'd* means 'engraved in fine lines,' and seems to refer to Nestor's silver hair. Dr. Johnson, however, thought that a contrast with Agamemnon's speech was intended—that one should be engraved in brass, the symbol of force and strength, the other in silver, the symbol of gentleness and persuasiveness.

I. iii. 73. *mastic*. Perhaps an adjective formed from *mastix*, a scourge, with a possible punning allusion to Dekker's railing play, *Satiromastix* (1602). Another explanation is that mastic gum was used as a remedy for aching teeth, and that there is a reference here to Thersites' ugliness of feature. Rowe, followed by some modern editors, emended the word to *mastiff*, which was often spelled 'mastie' or 'masty.'

I. iii. 75-137. J. H. Hanford shows (*Studies in Philology*, 13. 100-109) that while the germ of this speech may be found in Chapman's *Iliads* (II, 169-175), as has been stated, the aristocratic idea of government which Ulysses expresses was almost universal during the renaissance and found its ultimate source in Plato's *Republic*, LeRoy's French version of which was published in 1600. The idea is further developed in *Henry V*, I. ii. 178-213.

I. iii. 92. *aspects.* The aspect of a planet, according to astrology, is its position with reference to the other planets. Its influence depends upon this relative position.

I. iii. 113. *sop.* 'A mere pulp.' A sop is a piece of bread or something of the sort steeped and softened in liquor.

I. iii. 119, 120. *Then everything includes itself in power, Power into will, will into appetite.* 'Then everything resolves itself into power, power, in its turn, resolves itself into will, etc.' (Deighton.)

I. iii. 127-129. *And this neglection . . . climb.* 'This neglect of rank results in pushing backward step by step those who try to use it for the purpose of climbing upward.'

I. iii. 143. *forehand.* Originally a term in archery for an arrow used against a target directly in front of, and at a fixed distance from, the archer. In contrast to the 'forehand shaft' was the 'rover,' used in more informal shooting.

I. iii. 145. *Grows dainty of his worth.* 'Sets too great store by his prowess, so that he will not exert it on our behalf.'

I. iii. 157. *o'er-wrested.* A wrest was a peg used for tuning stringed instruments.

I. iii. 160. *Typhon.* A terrible giant with a hundred heads who attempted to overthrow Jupiter, but was subdued by him with a thunderbolt and imprisoned under Mount Ætna. He was sometimes called Typhœus.

I. iii. 167, 168. *as near as the extremest ends Of parallels, as like as Vulcan and his wife.* Not at all near or like, since the ends of parallels do not meet, and Vulcan's wife was Venus.

I. iii. 180. *Severals and generals of grace exact.*

'Qualities and excellencies which we possess as individuals or as a group.'

I. iii. 202, 203. *and know by measure Of their
observant toil the enemies' weight.* 'Know the enemies' strength exactly by means of laborious observa-
tion.'

I. iii. 212. *Makes many Thetis' sons.* 'Makes all
men equal in strength.' Nestor means that if the
estimate of the value of strategy which Ulysses has
just quoted is accepted it makes all men of equal value
provided that they have equal amounts of physical
force at their disposal.

I. iii. 228. *on.* This is the Folio reading. The
Quarto reading, *bid,* is frequently adopted by modern
editors.

I. iii. 238, 239. *and, Jove's accord, Nothing so full
of heart.* These lines may be corrupt and have been
much emended. The most satisfactory interpretation
seems to be, 'when they have the accord of Jove on
their side, nothing is so courageous as the Trojans.'
(Steevens.)

I. iii. 293. *host.* The Folio reads *mould,* but the
Quarto reading here given is generally adopted.

I. iii. 301. *prove.* This is another generally accepted reading from the Quarto. The Folio reads
pawn.

I. iii. 313. *Be you my time to bring it to some shape.*
'Be to my conception what time is to the embryo.'
(Deighton.)

I. iii. 316-319. *the seeded pride . . . evil.*
Achilles' pride is compared to a plant grown to such
maturity that it is about to go to seed. It must be
cut down before the seeds are dispersed and produce
a great crop of similar plants.

I. iii. 339-346. *Our . . . large.* 'Our reputation
will be curiously well weighed in this action, for its
outcome, although it primarily concerns only one in-

dividual, will give a specimen of our general success or failure, and in such tables of contents, though mere dots in comparison with the volumes which follow them, may be seen a tiny representation of the great things which are to follow.'

I. iii. 351-356. *who miscarrying . . . limbs.* 'If he fails, what encouragement does the conquering side receive from that to strengthen their good opinion of themselves? If this belief is entertained it will direct the limbs of those who hold it no less than their limbs direct their swords and bows.'

I. iii. 378. *Myrmidon.* The Myrmidons were the Thessalian followers of Achilles, who was known as 'the great Myrmidon.'

II. i. 9. *matter.* A quibble on the two meanings, *pus* and *sense.*

II. i. 14. *mongrel.* According to Caxton, Telamon had carried off to Greece Priam's sister, Hesione, who became the mother of Ajax. He was, therefore, half Greek and half Trojan. Cf. II. ii. 77.

II. i. 15. *vinewed'st.* The Folio spelling of this word is 'whinid'st.' The Quarto has *thou unsalted leaven.*

II. i. 37. *Cerberus.* The three-headed dog which guarded the gate of Hades. Proserpina was the wife of Pluto, the God of the Lower World.

II. i. 46. *stool for a witch.* A vituperative, and probably obscene, expression of uncertain meaning.

II. i. 115. *your.* Theobald's emendation of *their* in both Folio and Quarto.

II. i. 119, 120. *To Achilles, to Ajax, to—.* This is the reading of both Folio and Quarto which modern editors usually punctuate, *To, Achilles! to, Ajax! to! To* was the usual cry of encouragement to a fighting dog.

II. i. 126. *brach.* Rowe's emendation of *brooch* of

both Folio and Quarto. This emendation is accepted by most modern editors.

II. ii. 16. *tent.* A roll of lint used for probing deep wounds.

II. ii. 19, 20. *Every tithe soul, 'mongst many thousand dismes, Hath been as dear as Helen.* 'Every soul that has been taken as a tithe by the war is as dear as Helen, and of such tithes there have been many thousands.' (Deighton.)

II. ii. 28. *counters.* Part of the abacus which was used for calculating as late as Shakespeare's day. Troilus means that Priam's greatness cannot be measured by any ordinary standards.

II. ii. 29. *The past proportion of his infinite.* 'The infinite magnitude of his immeasurable greatness.'

II. ii. 33. *reasons.* This word was pronounced like *raisins* and Helenus is here punning.

II. ii. 38. *You fur your gloves with reason.* 'You line your speech with reason as gloves are lined with fur.' (Deighton.)

II. ii. 45. *And fly like chidden Mercury from Jove.* This line is misplaced in the Folio, where it occurs after l. 46 of this edition. The passage is correctly printed in the Quarto.

II. ii. 53. *particular will.* 'The arbitrary value which a particular person puts upon an object.'

II. ii. 58-60. 'The desire is foolish which inclines toward what it unwholesomely longs for, if there is no sign that the worth exists which is the ground of the longing.' (Tatlock.)

II. ii. 67, 68. *There can be no evasion To blench from this and to stand firm by honour.* 'There can be no subterfuge which will enable me to shrink from a choice I have made and still maintain my honor.'

II. ii. 70. *soil'd.* This is the reading of the Quarto which is generally accepted. The Folio reading is *spoil'd.*

II. ii. 71. *sieve.* This is the reading of the Quarto. The Folio reading, *same,* appears to be a misprint.

II. ii. 72-79. *It was thought meet . . . morning.* When Priam, angered at the treatment of Hesione by Telamon (see note on II. i. 14), proposed an expedition against the Greeks to recover her and take vengeance on her captors, Paris told the story of his judgment of the goddesses and Venus's promise of the fairest wife in Greece. He suggested that he lead an expedition to Greece which should seize Hesione if possible, but which should, at all events, bring back a Greek queen as a captive to atone for the ravishment of Priam's sister. This plan having been approved, Paris set out, and took advantage of the hospitality of Menelaus to carry off his wife. The natural indignation of the Greeks resulted in the Trojan war.

II. ii. 81, 82. *Why, she is a pearl, Whose price hath launch'd above a thousand ships.* These lines are based on the famous cry, 'Is this the face that launched a thousand ships?', with which Doctor Faustus, in Marlowe's play of that name, greeted the beauty of Helen of Troy.

II. ii. 90. *And do a deed that Fortune never did.* 'And act with more caprice than Fortune ever did.'

II. ii. 95, 96. *That in their country did them that disgrace We fear to warrant in our native place.* 'Who in their country (i.e. Greece) did them an injury which we fear to justify or defend in our own country.'

II. ii. 110. *firebrand.* Before the birth of Paris, Hecuba dreamed that she would be delivered of a burning torch which would destroy the city. Consequently the baby Paris was exposed on a mountain to perish, but was found and adopted by a shepherd who brought him up.

II. ii. 166, 167. *whom Aristotle thought Unfit to hear moral philosophy.* Aristotle, in *Nicomachean Ethics,* remarks that young men are not fit to study

political philosophy. Proponents of the Baconian
theory have made much of the fact that Bacon makes
the same error in his *Advancement of Learning*. Sir
Sidney Lee, however, has shown that this interpretation of Aristotle's words was usual in the sixteenth
and seventeenth centuries. He finds it in at least five
other places.

II. ii. 172. *adders.* The belief that adders deaf-
ened themselves by stopping their ears is at least as
old as the Psalms. Deighton quotes an apposite passage from the *Sermons* of Wyclif: 'But Christ biddeth
his disciples be prudent as adders. An adder hath
this wit; when charmers come to take him, the one of
his ears he clappeth to the earth, and with the end of
his tail he stoppeth the other.' Cf. Shakespeare's
one hundred and twelfth *Sonnet: that my adder's sense
To critic and to flatterer stopped are.*

II. iii. 20. *Neapolitan.* The disease was supposed
to have originated in Naples. This word does not
occur in the Folio.

II. iii. 27-29. *If . . . contemplation.* Thersites
is playing on the word *slip* which meant a counterfeit
coin of brass coated with silver.

II. iii. 45. *cheese.* Cheese was generally believed
to aid the process of digestion.

II. iii. 87. *shent.* Theobald's emendation of the
Folio reading, *sent.* The Quarto has *sate.*

II. iii. 89. *told so, lest.* This is the Quarto reading.
The Folio has *told of, so.*

II. iii. 90. *We dare not move the question of our
place.* 'We dare not bring up the subject of our position by asserting authority.'

II. iii. 104-107. Nestor and Ulysses are playing on
the word *argument.* Nestor says that Ajax will lack
material for railing since Achilles has taken from him
the subject of this railing. Ulysses denies this statement on the ground that Achilles, who now has Ajax's

former 'argument' (Thersites), has himself become the subject of his railing.

II. iii. 114-116. *The elephant . . . flexure.* The belief that the elephant had no joints was an 'old and grey-headed error,' being derived from Ctesias, the first Greek to see and describe such an animal. The idea was controverted by Aristotle, and was later dealt with by Sir Thomas Browne in his *Pseudodoxia Epidemica. Flexure* is the Quarto reading. The Folio has *flight,* which seems to be wrong in this context.

II. iii. 135. *note of judgment.* 'The distinctive trait of judgment,' or, perhaps, 'In the observant opinion of people capable of judging.'

II. iii. 140. *lines.* This word survives in the Warwickshire dialect in the expression 'on a line,' meaning 'in a rage.' Cf. also *The Merry Wives of Windsor* (IV. ii. 21, 22), *Your husband is in his old lines again.* Hanmer, followed by many modern editors, emended the word to *lunes,* whims or caprices coming from the influence of the moon, thus carrying out the figure of the tide. The reading of the Quarto is *His course and time.*

II. iii. 177. *Without observance or respect of any.* 'Without regarding or considering the wishes of others.'

II. iii. 184. *worth.* This is the reading of the Quarto and seems to be correct. The Folio reading is *wroth.*

II. iii. 189. *death-tokens.* Spots, believed to be indicative of approaching death, which appeared on the bodies of those sick with the plague.

II. iii. 208, 209. *And add . . . Hyperion.* 'Add more heat to the summer.' The sun (Hyperion) enters the sign Cancer at the summer solstice.

II. iii. 234. *A' would have ten shares.* This is an allusion to the practice of dividing the proprietary rights in Elizabethan theatres into shares. On February 21, 1599, the property of the Globe was so divided into ten shares, of which Shakespeare held one. (See C. W. Wallace, 'Shakespeare's Money Interest in the Globe Theatre,' *Century Magazine,* LVIII, 506-509.) Will Kempe, another shareholder, quarreled with his associates, and Professor Wallace thinks that this line is an allusion to that episode. Ulysses here means that Ajax would have not half, but all, the pride in the world.   The allusion offers some evidence for the date of composition of the play.

II. iii. 236. *He's not yet through warm.* This line is continued to Ajax in the Folio.   Theobald, probably correctly, assigned it to Nestor.

II. iii. 261. *Milo.* Milo of Crotona was renowned for having carried a bull on his shoulders through the stadium at Olympia.   The incident is described in Cicero's *De Senectute.*   This is another of the frequent anachronisms in Shakespeare, like the reference to Aristotle (II. ii. 166), for Milo lived in the sixth century, B.C., long after the Trojan war.

II. iii. 280. *boats sail.* The Folio reading is *boats may sail,* which destroys the metre.   This is the reading of the Quarto.

III. i. 13-18. 'The servant means to quibble.   He hopes that Pandarus will become a better man than he is at present.   In his next speech he chooses to understand Pandarus as if he had said he wished to grow better, and hence the servant affirms that he is in a state of grace.'   (Malone.)   Pandarus carries on the quibble by taking the word 'grace' as a title of nobility which is too high for his rank.

III. i. 36. *love's invisible soul.* This probably means, 'the soul of love, invisible except when personified in the beauty of Helen.'

III. i. 45, 46. *stewed phrase.* There is probably a quibble on the word *seethes,* with an allusion in *sodden* to the 'sweating-tub' cure for venereal disease and in *stewed* to the stews or brothels.

III. i. 97. *disposer.* This may mean, 'one who disposes or inclines me to mirth by her pleasant (and rather free) talk.' Dyce thus explains the word and gives instances of its use in this sense.

III. i. 119. *fine forehead.* The point of this remark is not clear. Possibly the forehead was believed to indicate musical talent.

III. i. 132. *sore.* Wound, with a play on the word in its other meaning, a three-year-old buck.

III. i. 174. *Sweet, above thought I love thee.* Continued to Helen in the Folio. The reading of the Quarto, here given, seems to be correct.

III. ii. 10. *Charon.* Charon was the ferryman who transported souls across the river Styx.

III. ii. 21. *repured.* This is the reading of the Quarto. The Folio reading, *reputed,* appears to be a misprint.

III. ii. 43. *watch'd.* Hawks were tamed by being 'watched,' or kept awake. Pandarus thinks that Cressida should be treated in this way.

III. ii. 47. *draw this curtain.* 'Remove your veil.' In Shakespeare's time paintings were often protected by curtains which could be drawn aside to show the picture.

III. ii. 50. *rub on, and kiss the mistress.* 'Overcome all obstacles and reach the goal.' In bowls the *jack* or *mistress* was the goal, and *to rub* referred to meeting obstacles on the way.

III. ii. 51. *fee-farm.* A fee-farm was a grant of land in perpetuity, a certain rent being reserved.

III. ii. 53, 54. *The falcon as the tercel, for all the ducks i' th' river.* Pandarus means that he will back Cressida to hold her own with Troilus. The female hawk, or falcon, and the male, or tercel, were used in duck hunting.

III. ii. 59, 60. *'In witness whereof the parties in-terchangeably.'* The first half of a legal formula which was completed by the words, 'have set their hands and seals.' The figure of a kiss as a (legal) seal of love was a common conceit in Elizabethan poetry.

III. ii. 103, 104. *as what envy can say worst shall be a mock for his truth.* 'The worst thing that malice can do to him will be to sneer at him for his constancy.'

III. ii. 140. *Cunning.* This is Pope's plausible emendation of *Comming* in both Folio and Quarto.

III. ii. 168. *in plight and youth.* 'In good condition and the freshness of youth.'

III. ii. 184. *plantage.* There was an old belief that the growth of vegetation was influenced by the increase of the moon.

III. ii. 215, 216. *Whereupon I will show you a chamber whose bed.* The reading of both Folio and Quarto is *Whereupon I will show you a chamber, which bed.* The present reading is a conjecture by Dyce.

III. ii. 217. *press.* This is an allusion to the practice of punishing murderers who refused to plead by pressing them to death with weights.

III. iii. 4. *That through the sight I bear in things to love.* This is a difficult line for which many emendations have been proposed. It probably means, 'Through my insight and peculiar perception of things which should be loved.'

III. iii. 20. *have you thanks.* This is the reading of the Quarto. The Folio has, *have you, thanks.*

III. iii. 21. *in right great exchange.* 'In exchange for prisoners on whom the Trojans set great store.'

III. iii. 30. *In most accepted pain.* 'In hardships and pains which I have most willingly accepted.'

III. iii. 84-87. *Which when they fall . . . fall.* 'These prizes, since they are not on a firm basis, and the equally unstable friendships that rest on them, pull down each other when the prizes fall and perish as a result.'

III. iii. 95. *strange fellow.* Grant White pointed out that the 'strange fellow' is probably Plato, since Ulysses' quotation resembles closely a passage in the *First Alcibiades.* Shakespeare may have read Plato in a Latin translation.

III. iii. 110. *married.* This is the reading of both Folio and Quarto. Many modern editors follow Collier's MS. in emending the word to *mirror'd.*

III. iii. 125. *The unknown Ajax.* Clarke suggests that this line means that Ajax was 'unknown to himself, wanting in true self-knowledge,' Johnson that he is 'one who has abilities which were never brought into play or use.' Ulysses seems to be flattering Ajax by suggesting that there are profound qualities in his nature which do not appear.

III. iii. 134, 135. *How some men creep in skittish Fortune's hall, Whiles others play the idiots in her eyes!* 'How some men creep about in capricious Fortune's hall, without making themselves conspicuous, while others constantly strive to attract her attention by playing the idiot.'

III. iii. 146. *alms for oblivion.* Oblivion is here personified as a monster who lives on the reputations of men provided for him by Time. Great names are gathered into Time's wallet and handed over to oblivion, who devours them.

III. iii. 162. *abject rear.* The Folio reading is *abject, near,* which was plausibly emended to the present reading by Hanmer. This meaning of *abject,* which occurs again in l. 128 of this scene, is somewhat unusual (see *New Eng. Dict.,* s.v., *abject*). There is no implication that the rear was cowardly and in flight, but rather that it was despicable in being in the rear rather than in the front of the battle. The application of the lines is that Achilles will be trampled on by less worthy and less courageous men than himself when they do come up, just as the gallant horse is trampled on by those of the rear which lack the courage to make them fight in the front rank. The 'abject' reap the benefit of the courage and sacrifice of the brave. These lines do not appear in the Quarto.

III. iii. 175. *One touch of nature makes the whole world kin.* This is one of the most frequently misapplied lines from Shakespeare. It is, of course, the trait of loving novelty that is common to everyone and makes the whole world kin.

III. iii. 178. *give.* This emendation of *go,* the reading of both Folio and Quarto, was proposed by Thirlby and first adopted by Theobald. It is now universally accepted.

III. iii. 183. *sooner.* This is the Quarto reading. The Folio reading is *begin to.*

III. iii. 184. *once.* This is the Quarto reading. The Folio reading is *out.*

III. iii. 189, 190. *Made emulous missions 'mongst the gods themselves, And drave great Mars to faction.* 'Made the gods give up their impartial attitude and forced Mars to take sides.'

III. iii. 193, 194. *'Tis known, Achilles, that you are in love With one of Priam's daughters.* The story of Achilles and Polyxena is told by both Lydgate and Caxton. Achilles fell in love with Polyxena and obtained the permission of Priam and Hecuba to marry her on condition that he bring about peace. His effort to do so failed and, shutting himself in his tent, he gave himself over to melancholy. After a series of Greek victories and the death of Patroclus he was persuaded to take the field and soon afterwards slew Hector. Hecuba thereupon sent for him to come to the Temple of Apollo to discuss his marriage with Polyxena and there had Paris slay him treacherously

to avenge the death of Hector. At the end of the war
the Greeks were delayed by unfavorable winds until,
at the insistence of Calchas, they sacrificed Polyxena to
Achilles, thus procuring atonement for his murder
by her brother.

III. iii. 198. *Pluto's.* Shakespeare seems to have
confused Plutus, the God of Wealth, with Pluto, the
God of the Lower World. Some such confusion, however, existed in classical times.

III. iii. 200, 201. *Keeps place with thought, and
almost, like the gods, Does thoughts unveil in their
dumb cradles.* 'Such foresight is everywhere present,
even where thoughts are conceived and developed.'

III. iii. 216. *The fool slides o'er the ice that you
should break.* 'This curious conceit seems to be made
clear by none of the commentators, and to be ignored
by almost all. Halliwell-Phillipps pointed out in
1883 that it alludes to a quaint anecdote first published
in 1605 and 1608 (see *A Nest of Ninnies,* pp. 37,
38; Shakespeare Society, 1842), which Shakespeare
doubtless heard from the writer of it, Robert Armin, a
member of his company from 1599 to 1603. A half-
witted country-fellow, stage-struck, escaped from his
confinement, and, to follow Armin's company, passed
safely over an expanse of ice so thin that a brickbat
dropped on it broke through. Ulysses' meaning
clearly is, "You should break the thin ice Ajax is
sliding over, and so keep him in his own place." '
(Tatlock.) Another possible interpretation is, 'The
fool (Ajax) can run risks which would be fatal to, or
unworthy of, a man of your dignity and position.' The
line offers additional evidence of the date of composition of the play.

III. iii. 229. *shrewdly gor'd.* Achilles is carrying
on the figure from the sport of bull-baiting implied in
the words *at stake* in the previous line.

III. iii. 232. *Seals a commission to a blank of*

danger. 'Puts one at the mercy of an unknown danger.' A blank commission was sometimes sealed and given to an agent of the crown to fill out as he chose, thus giving him complete power over a helpless victim.

III. iii. 245, 246. *Ajax goes up and down the field, asking for himself.* Here Thersites makes the very popular Elizabethan pun on *Ajax* and *a jakes,* a privy, which was based on similarity of pronunciation. The pun may appear elsewhere in the play, but this is the only place at which it is certainly intended.

IV. i. 16. *But when contention and occasion meets.* 'But when the opportune time for fighting comes.'

IV. i. 22. *Venus' hand.* Venus was the mother of Æneas. Warburton thought that Æneas was alluding resentfully to the fact that Diomedes had wounded Venus in the hand when she took part in the war. He may, however, be simply swearing first by his father and then by his mother.

IV. i. 62. *tamed piece.* 'A wine-cask that has been long open, so that its contents have become flat.' He refers to a woman who has lost her virtue and charm.

IV. i. 66. *But he as he, which heavier for a whore.* This is the reading of the Folio. The Quarto reading, *the heavier,* is frequently adopted by modern editors. The meaning of the line clearly is that there is nothing to choose between Menelaus and Paris, that their deserts are exactly balanced by their attitudes toward Helen and their relations with her.

IV. i. 78. *We'll not commend what we intend to sell.* 'We, unlike the merchants, will be modest about our commodities.' This line seems to have a sense opposite to the logical one, and may have been corrupted. Many editors emend it to, *We'll but commend what we intend to sell.*

IV. ii. 4. *kill.* If this word is correct, it is a hyperbole for *subdue* or *overpower.* Various emendations have been proposed, among them *still, seal, fill,* and *kiss.*

IV. ii. 13. *tediously.* This is the reading of the Quarto. The Folio reading, *hideously,* appears to be a misprint.

IV. ii. 109. *extremes.* This is the reading of the Quarto. The Folio reading, *extremity,* destroys the metre.

IV. iii. 11. *And would, as I shall pity, I could help.* 'And wish I could help you as truly as I shall pity you.'

IV. iv. 4. *violenteth.* This is the reading of the Quarto. The Folio has *no less in a sense.*

IV. iv. 24. *strain'd.* This is the reading of the Quarto. The Folio has *strange.*

IV. iv. 45. *With distinct breath and consign'd kisses to them.* 'Each distinct, with a pause, or breath, allotted to each of the numerous farewells.'

IV. iv. 50. *Genius.* The tutelary spirit of Roman mythology which watched over a man through life and finally summoned him to death.

IV. iv. 57. *When shall we see again?* This line is given to Troilus in the Folio and, probably correctly, to Cressida in the Quarto.

IV. iv. 60, 61. *Nay, we must use expostulation kindly, For it is parting from us.* 'We must not plead with each other unkindly, for we must part now and the opportunity for pleading will not be ours much longer.'

IV. iv. 63, 64. *For I will throw my glove to Death himself, That there's no maculation in thy heart.* 'My conviction of your fidelity would make me challenge Death himself if he doubted it.'

IV. iv. 65, 66. *to fashion in My sequent protestation.* 'To foreshadow or introduce the protestation I am about to make.' 'Be thou true' is the introduction, 'And I will see thee,' the conclusion.

IV. iv. 77, 78. *They're loving, well compos'd, with gift of nature, Flowing and swelling o'er with arts and exercise.* This is Staunton's reading, based on the Folio, which is generally accepted by modern editors. The Folio reading is *Their loving well compos'd, with gift of nature, Flawing and swelling o'er with arts and exercise.*

IV. iv. 86. *lavolt.* The lavolt, or lavolta, was a lively dance with much 'lofty jumping.'

IV. iv. 103, 104. *Whiles others fish with craft for great opinion, I with great truth catch mere simplicity.* 'While some men use all their craft to gain great fame, I, because of my plain truth, have the reputation of a simple, straightforward man.'

IV. iv. 122, 123. *To shame the zeal of my petition to thee In praising her.* The Folio reading is *To shame the seal of my petition towards, I praising her.* Warburton first emended *seal* to *zeal;* the rest is the reading of the Quarto.

IV. iv. 132. *I'll answer to my lust.* Various emendations have been proposed for this line. Deighton suggests that the compositor caught the *'ll* from the line below and that Diomedes said, 'I answer to my lust,' i.e., 'When I am at home I speak out plainly, and I ask for the same privilege here.'

IV. v. 8. *bias cheek.* 'Swelling out like the bias of a bowl.' (Johnson.) Steevens thought that the idea was taken from the puffed cheeks of the winds as represented in old maps.

IV. v. 59. *coasting.* The meaning of this word is uncertain. Theobald and many modern editors emend *a coasting* to *accosting.*

IV. v. 62. *sluttish spoils of opportunity.* 'Wanton women whose virtue may be easily conquered whenever opportunity offers.'

IV. v. 78-81. *In the extremity . . . nothing.* 'In the extreme greatness of his valour, as in the extreme littleness of his pride, Hector is pre-eminent.' (Deighton.)　The one quality is almost infinite, the other almost non-existent.

IV. v. 96.　The Folio here reads, *The youngest son of Priam, a true knight; they call him Troilus.*　This is clearly an error of the compositor, who picked up the last clause from below.

IV. v. 105, 106.　*in his blaze of wrath, subscribes To tender objects.*　'Although his anger is white hot, yields mercy when there is an occasion for tenderness.'

IV. v. 141.　*Neoptolemus.*　Perhaps Pyrrhus Neoptolemus, the son of Achilles, who later, according to Caxton, became a great hero among the Greek warriors.　Johnson, however, thought that Shakespeare took Neoptolemus to be the family name and here meant Achilles himself.　This view may be correct, as Pyrrhus has not yet become distinguished and as he is previously (III. iii. 210) said to be at home.

IV. v. 142.　*Oyes. Oyez,* 'hear ye.'　The demand for attention which preceded a public proclamation.

IV. v. 155.　*To the expecters of our Troyan part.* 'To those of our Trojan party who are waiting to hear the result of this encounter.'

IV. v. 162, 163.　*as welcome as to one That would be rid of such an enemy.*　'As welcome as you could be to one who would gladly be rid of such an enemy as you are.'

IV. v. 168.　*Strain'd purely from all hollow bias-drawing.*　'Purged entirely of all swerving such as is given to the movement of the bowl by the bias.'　Cf. note on I. iii. 13-17.

IV. v. 183.　*Labouring for destiny.*　'Acting on behalf of destiny (by killing so many of the enemy).'

IV. v. 186.　*scorning forfeits and subduements.* 'Not bothering with those whose lives were already forfeited and who were already subdued.'

V. i. 12, 13. *The surgeon's box, or the patient's wound.* Thersites wilfully misunderstands Patroclus and puns on the two senses of the word *tent.* Cf. II. ii. 16.

V. i. 35. *sleave silk.* This is the Quarto reading. The Folio has *sleyd silk.*

V. i. 59-61. *the goodly transformation . . . cuckolds.* Jupiter transformed himself into a white bull in order to win, or to abduct, Europa. Having horns, he was, according to Thersites, a symbol of Menelaus, the prototype and perverse emblem of cuckolds.

V. i. 101, 102. *He will spend his mouth, and promise, like Brabbler the hound.* 'He will give tongue when he is not on the scent of a fox.' Hounds with this failing were, and still are, called 'brabblers.'

V. ii. 10, 11. *any man may sing her, if he can take her cliff.* This is the reading of the Quarto and has the play on the words of the preceding speech which is demanded by the punning use of *noted.* The Folio reading is *any man may find her if he can take her life.*

V. ii. 21. *tell a pin.* The pin was regarded as the type of insignificance, and this expression, or a similar one, was proverbially used to express impatience with trifles or to cut short any attempt at evasion.

V. ii. 41. *all hell's.* So the Quarto. The Folio has *hell.*

V. ii. 54. *potato finger.* Potatoes, especially sweet potatoes, and dates were believed to stimulate sexual desire.

V. ii. 78. *Nay, do not snatch it from me.* These words are given to Diomed in both Folio and Quarto. This change, suggested by Thirlby and first adopted by Theobald, seems to be correct.

V. ii. 79. *doth take.* This is the reading of the

Quarto. The Folio reading, *takes* (or *rakes*), destroys the metre.

V. ii. 99, 100. *Nor I, by Pluto; but that that likes not me Pleases me best.* Thersites does not approve of Cressida's attitude, but at the same time he gets a malignant pleasure from her treatment of Diomed and from the general situation.

V. ii. 110. *A proof of strength she could not publish more.* 'A strong proof of her own character which she could not publish more clearly.'

V. ii. 119. *th' attest.* So the Quarto. The Folio has *that test.*

V. ii. 138. *If there be rule in unity itself.* 'If there be a natural law that one person must be himself and no one else.' (Tatlock.)

V. ii. 139-143. *O madness . . . revolt.* 'O mad reasoning, which sets up a debate both for and against itself; a double authority where reason can revolt against itself without the loss (perdition) of any of its essential virtue, and yet can assume lost reason to be reasonable without revolting against itself.' Briefly, 'reason can be a traitor to itself without the sacrifice of its innate virtue.'

V. ii. 141. *Bi-fold.* This is the Quarto reading. The Folio, evidently wrongly, has *By foule.*

V. ii. 149. *Ariachne's.* Arachne wove a web so fine that her rival, Pallas, destroyed it in a fit of anger and changed the weaver into a spider. 'Ariachne's broken woof' means the spider's web. Shakespeare seems to confuse the name of Arachne with that of Ariadne who gave Theseus the thread to guide him out of the labyrinth of Crete.

V. ii. 158, 159. *May worthy Troilus be half attach'd With that which here his passion doth express?* 'Can worthy Troilus be even one half as strongly affected as his passion here would indicate?'

V. ii. 164. *much as I.* The word *as* is omitted in both Folio and Quarto.

V. ii. 170. *sun.* This is the Quarto reading. The Folio has *Fenne,* which is a natural misprint.

V. ii. 191. *parrot will not do more for an almond.* The parrot's fondness for almonds was proverbial and is frequently referred to in Elizabethan literature.

V. iii. 6. *ominous to the day.* 'Prophetic of the sorrows which the day will bring forth.'

V. iii. 21. *For we would give much, to use violent thefts.* 'Because we wish to give much in charity, to get the means for doing so by violent theft.' This reading is Tyrwhitt's and is generally accepted. The reading of the Folio is *For we would count give much to as violent thefts.* The line does not appear in the Quarto.

V. iii. 26. *keeps the weather of.* 'Keeps to windward of.' A nautical term meaning 'to have the advantage over.'

V. iii. 38. *lion.* The lion was traditionally believed to act with mercy and generosity toward those who humbled themselves before him.

V. iii. 69. *in the faith of valour.* 'By the honour of a brave man.' (Deighton.) *Noblesse oblige.*

V. iii. 110. *Th' effect doth operate another way.* 'The effect of the letter is not to show what she feels in her heart, but something quite different.'

V. iii. 114-116. *Why . . . name.* These lines occur again, with a slight variation, at V. x. 32-34 in the Folio. In the Quarto they appear only in the latter place. This repetition indicates some sort of revision or confusion.

V. iv. 13. *set me up.* Set up in opposition. *Me* is the weak 'ethical dative' which appears frequently in Shakespeare.

V. iv. 18. *to proclaim barbarism.* 'To set up the

authority of ignorance, to declare that they will be governed by policy no longer.' (Johnson.)

V. iv. 23, 24. *advantageous care Withdrew me from the odds of multitude.* 'Prudent care for my life caused me to withdraw from battle against overwhelming numbers.'

V. v. 14. *Sagittary.* Caxton thus describes the Sagittary: 'a mervayllous beste that was called *sagittayre,* that behinde the myddes was an horse, and to fore a man: this beste was heery like an horse, and had his eyen rede as a cole, and shotte well with a bowe: this beste made the Greekes sore aferde, and slew many of them with his bowe.' The creature is also described in detail by Lydgate.

V. vii. 6. *In fellest manner execute your arms.* The word *arms* in this line was emended by Capell to *aims,* and most modern editors have adopted his reading. An obsolete sense of the word *execute* is, however, 'to make use of, or bring into operation, a weapon.' See *New Eng. Dict.,* s.v., *execute.*

V. vii. 11. *double-henn'd sparrow.* Thersites apparently refers to Paris as a sparrow which has a double hen—double in the senses of having two husbands and of being false.

V. viii. 18. *stickler-like.* A stickler was an umpire at a duel. He stood by with a staff to part the duellists if the issue could be decided without bloodshed.

V. viii. 20. *bait.* This is the reading of the Quarto. The Folio has *bed.*

V. x. 13, 14. *But dare all imminence that gods and men Address their dangers in.* 'But dare whatever imminent dangers either gods or men may be preparing for me.' (Deighton.)

V. x. 55. *galled goose of Winchester.* 'A sufferer from venereal disease who might be galled by Pandarus' words.' The stews in Southwark were licensed by and under the jurisdiction of the Bishop of Win-

chester. A 'Winchester Goose' was also the cant term
for a kind of sore.

V. x. 56. *sweat.* An allusion to a common cure for
venereal disease.

APPENDIX A

Sources of the Play

The plot of *Troilus and Cressida* falls into two closely interwoven parts, the one concerned with the history of the love of Troilus and Cressida and the other dealing with the incidents of the siege of Troy. The ultimate sources of these divisions of the play are definitely known. The story of Troilus and Cressida is largely adapted from Chaucer's long narrative poem, *Troilus and Criseyde;* the scenes which treat of the Greek and Trojan warriors are mainly based on Caxton's *Recuyell of the Historyes of Troy,* a translation from the French of Raoul Lefévre's *Recueil des Histoires de Troie.* The story as it appears in Caxton goes back in a direct line from Lefévre through Guido delle Colonne and Benoît de Sainte-More to Dares and Dictys, whose accounts of the siege pretended to be those of actual participants in it. Both narratives were actually written in the early centuries of the Christian era. The story of Troilus and his love appears first in Benoît and may be presumed to have been invented by him. Boccaccio borrowed the story to form the subject of his *Il Filostrato,* and Chaucer, in turn, based his version of the history of the two lovers on Boccaccio's poem. Lydgate's *Troy Book* may also have provided material for Shakespeare's play, and Chapman's translation of seven books of the *Iliad,* published in 1598, undoubtedly furnished important hints, particularly for the character of Thersites. As the play, however, seems to refer to incidents from parts of the *Iliad* not included in the 1598 edition of Chapman's translation, further hints may have been drawn from the several available translations of Homer in French and Latin or from an earlier English version of the first ten books of the *Iliad.*

Troilus and Cressida seems to bear some direct relation to the First Part of Thomas Heywood's *The Iron Age,* a play dealing with the same material, but as the similarity between the plays lies in the arrangement of incident and in general tone rather than in verbal resemblances, direct borrowing by one from the other seems unlikely. *The Iron Age,* which was a popular play for a number of years, was written for a rival company, so that if it was earlier than or contemporary with *Troilus and Cressida* the manuscript would hardly have been available to Shakespeare at the time that he was working on his play. If, as Professor Adams suggests,[1] *The Iron Age* was written about 1610-1612 and was acted at that time by the combined companies of the Queen's Men, for whom it was written, and the King's Men, Shakespeare's company, *Troilus and Cressida* would have been available to Heywood in the Quarto, if in no other form. Since, however, there is so little indication of direct connection between the plays in important speeches and in verbal reminiscence, their relation is, in all probability, an indirect one.

The usually accepted explanation of this relation, as well as of the careless structure of the end of Shakespeare's play, is that an earlier play, perhaps by a University man who would be familiar with Homer and Chaucer and the various versions of the story of Troy, was rewritten by both Shakespeare and Heywood for immediate dramatic purposes. Critics are generally agreed that some one other than Shakespeare was concerned in the composition of the last scenes of *Troilus and Cressida* which do not much resemble the rest in quality, and which fail to tie up the main threads of the plot, so that the end of the play leaves an impression of weakness and lack of purpose. If

[1] Adams, J. Q., 'Shakespeare, Heywood, and the Classics,' *Modern Language Notes,* 34 (1919), 336.

Shakespeare was remodelling an old play he may easily have become negligent or hurried as he approached the end of his task so that the last scenes, by this theory, are substantially those of the original play. If it was decided not to produce the play at all, as is not unlikely, Shakespeare would naturally lay it aside and turn to more urgent work; if the play was to be produced, perhaps to compete with *The Iron Age* and a play on Troilus and Cressida which Dekker and Chettle wrote for Henslowe and the Admiral's Men in 1599, he may well have been so hurried that he could not complete his revision and left the final scenes much as he found them. The existence of such a source play cannot be proved unless a copy of it is found, but no other hypothesis of the kind so satisfactorily explains the relation of Shakespeare's play to its ultimate sources, its relation to *The Iron Age,* and the weakness of its final scenes. This explanation is, moreover, in entire accord with the practice of the dramatic writers of Elizabethan times.[1]

Such an explanation of the difficulties presented by *Troilus and Cressida* must, however, depend upon conjecture based upon evidence which is not always conclusive. It is at least possible that Shakespeare was entirely responsible for the play. He seems to have been familiar with Chaucer's poem, in which the Trojans appear as the refined and cultivated knights of the period of the decline of mediæval chivalry. In vivid contrast with this conception is the picture of the Greeks in Caxton and more particularly in Chapman, in whose versions of the story the Greek warriors are presented as rough, uncultured fighting men with none of the courtly grace of Chaucer's Trojans. This contrast is so sharply drawn in Shakespeare's play as

[1] See Tatlock, J. S. P., 'The Siege of Troy in Elizabethan Literature, especially in Shakespeare and Heywood,' *Publications of the Modern Language Association of America,* xxx (1915), 726-770.

to suggest that it may have been the basis of the author's original conception. If so, Shakespeare probably found that his material, in spite of several intensely dramatic episodes, was, on the whole, not dramatic, so that, losing interest at the end of the play, he brought it to a close in a few careless and hurried scenes.

The problem of the immediate origin of *Troilus and Cressida* cannot, then, be regarded as definitely settled unless more conclusive evidence is brought to light. It may have had to do with some minor outburst of professional rivalry among the theatrical companies of London, or it may have sprung directly from Shakespeare's reading and reflection on the legend of Troy. It may be found that the play is a reworking of an older theatrical version, or it may be that it came directly, with all its faults, from its author's mind.

APPENDIX B

The History of the Play

On February 7, 1603, the following entry was made in the Register of the Stationers' Company: 'Master Roberts. Entered for his copy in full Court holden this day to print when he hath gotten sufficient authority for it, The book of *Troilus and Cressida,* as it is acted by my lord Chamberlain's Men.' The Lord Chamberlain's Men, soon after to be known as the King's Men or the King's Majesty's Servants, were Shakespeare's company, and the play then licensed must have been his play, since it is most unlikely that two plays on the same subject and with the same title but by different authors would have been acted by a single company within the five or six years between the granting of this license and the publication of the Quarto in 1609. This entry was made by James Roberts, a printer friend of the actors who served them in this capacity more than once, probably in order to establish the copyright and block the unauthorized publication of the play in case a manuscript copy of it fell into the hands of some unscrupulous person. It was for the interest of the company to keep the play, probably then a new one, from publication as long as there was a chance of its being produced.

Nothing more is heard of the play until January 28, 1609, on which date another license was granted by the authorities, who apparently had forgotten or neglected the previous entry. At this time two young publishers, Bonian and Walley, were given authority to print 'a book called the history of Troylus and Cressida,' and not long afterwards, presumably, the quarto edition of the play was issued with the following title-page: 'The Historie of Troylus and Cresseida. As it was acted by the Kings Maiesties Seruants at the Globe. Written by William Shakespeare.' The statement that the play had been acted, as in the case of a similar statement in the licensing entry of 1603, may have been merely for the purpose of identifying the play and the company to which it belonged, and may not have been intended to be taken literally. It may, however, have been due to a misapprehension, for shortly afterwards another issue of the Quarto appeared containing both the prefatory epistle which stated that the play was a new one and had never been clapper-clawed with the palms of the vulgar, and a flamboyant new title-page which read: 'The Famous Historie of Troylus and Cresseid. Excellently expressing the beginning of their loues, with the conceited wooing of Pandarus Prince of Licia. Written by William Shakespeare.' Apparently after the publishers had issued a part of their edition, they discovered that the play had not been produced and hurried to make capital of this unusual circumstance in order to stimulate the sale of the book. Since the two issues of the Quarto are identical as to text, it is difficult otherwise to account for the new title-page and the epistle, although it has been suggested that the play was new only in a technical sense, having been revised from the acting version. It seems far more probable that the play had never been acted and that Bonian and Walley were at first unaware of that fact.

Troilus and Cressida was not again published, so far as is known, until it appeared in the Folio in 1623, at which time its publication seems to have been attended with many problems for the editors. It is not listed in the Catalogue of the plays at the beginning of the book and it is placed in a curious position between the histories and the tragedies. The original intention of the editors was to place it after *Romeo and Juliet,* but a difficulty evidently arose, perhaps over the copyright, and that place was given to *Timon of Athens.*

Part of *Troilus and Cressida* had already been printed, with the last lines of *Romeo and Juliet* on one side of the first leaf and the beginning of *Troilus and Cressida* on the other. The third and fourth pages, the only pages in the play to be numbered, bear the numbers 79 and 80, which would have been correct had the play been placed in the position first intended. When the difficulty was removed and the editors decided to include the play in its present position, the first leaf, containing the end of *Romeo and Juliet* and the beginning of *Troilus and Cressida,* was cancelled and replaced by a leaf which had the Prologue to *Troilus and Cressida* spread out in large italic type on one side and the beginning of the play on the other. Two copies of the Folio have survived in which the original cancelled leaf was accidentally included. Perhaps the editors were themselves unable to decide how the play should be classified. It is called a history on both title-pages of the Quarto, the prefatory epistle refers to it as a comedy, and the first three pages of the Folio version are headed, 'The Tragedy of Troylus and Cressida.' At any rate they placed the play in a neutral position, allowing the reader to do as he liked.[1]

The texts of the Folio and Quarto have numerous differences, and each includes lines which the other does not contain. The Folio text, although carelessly printed, is slightly preferable and the more complete of the two. A large number of the variants of the Quarto are merely correct printings of words misprinted in the Folio, but in several instances they are actually different readings. It is now believed that the Folio was printed from a manuscript belonging to the theatre and the Quarto from a copy made for the private use of some friend of the actors.

The entry in the Stationers' Register on February

[1] See Adams, J. Q., '*Timon of Athens* and the Irregularities in the First Folio,' *Journal of English and Germanic Philology,* vii (January, 1908), 53.

7, 1603, gives a later limit for the date of composition of the play: an earlier limit is suggested by several allusions in its text. The reference to the division of the shares of the Globe Theatre in February, 1599 (see note on II. iii. 234), would indicate that the play was composed after that date, and it is not likely that Shakespeare would have heard of the incident of the fool on the thin ice (see note on III. iii. 216) before Armin joined his company in the same year. Thersites' line, 'and devil Envy say Amen' (II. iii. 23), is probably an allusion to the use of Envy as one of the two Prologues to Ben Jonson's well-known *Poetaster* (produced about June, 1601), while the reference to the 'arm'd prologue' (Prol. 23, 24; see note) is probably an allusion to the other, in which the Prologue appeared defiantly in full armor. The reference to Thersites' 'mastic jaws' (I. iii. 73) may be an allusion to Dekker's *Satiromastix,* a popular railing play which appeared in August or September of 1601. All these allusions point to the years between 1599 and 1602 as the date of the composition of *Troilus and Cressida,* and their evidence is supported by the versification of the play which has the structural characteristics of the verse of this period of Shakespeare's artistic life.

It has been maintained by Fleay and others that Shakespeare revised his play several times during the fifteen years preceding the appearance of the Quarto, and that different parts of the play represent different periods of his development as a poet and a dramatist. This contention is, however, based on inconclusive evidence and seems to be without adequate foundation. It may be assumed with some confidence that the play was written in the latter part of 1601 or in 1602 in order to take advantage of the extraordinary interest in the Troy legend which was evinced by the literary world of London between 1599 and 1602, and, perhaps, to compete with the two rival plays on the same subject, Heywood's *The Iron Age* and the *Troilus and Cressida* of Dekker and Chettle.

Troilus and Cressida is among the least frequently acted of Shakespeare's plays. There is reason for believing that it was never performed during his lifetime, although the subject was enormously popular, and the first recorded performance after his death occurred in Munich in 1898. Since that performance there have been fifteen productions of the play. On the Continent it has been played in Berlin in 1899 and 1904, in Vienna in 1902, in Zürich in 1916, in Stuttgart in 1918 and 1920, in Leipzig in 1920, in Essen in 1923, and in Paris, in a French prose version, in 1912. There are only five recorded productions of the play in England. In 1907 it was performed in London under the direction of Mr. Charles Fry; in 1912 the Elizabethan Stage Society, under the direction of Mr. William Poel, presented the play in London and repeated their performance at the Shakespeare Memorial Theatre in Stratford in 1913; in 1922 it was performed in Cambridge and London by the Marlowe Society of Cambridge; and in 1923 the play completed the cycle of Shakespearean performances at the Old Vic in London. The only recorded production of the play in America occurred in 1916 when it was performed in Naugatuck and New Haven by the Yale University Dramatic Association under the direction of Mr. E. M. Woolley. John Kemble is said to have thought of producing the play, and Irving and others are believed to have made acting versions of it. After the Restoration, Dryden's adaptation of the play, called *Troilus and Cressida, or, Truth Found Too Late,* had some popularity, but for nearly three centuries Shakespeare's play seems never to have appeared on the stage.

APPENDIX C

The Authorship of the Play

Few, if any, critics question Shakespeare's authorship of any parts of the play except the Prologue and
Scenes iv-x of the Fifth Act, especially Scenes vii-x,
for Shakespeare's hand appears unmistakably at times
in Scenes iv-vi. On the whole, however, these last
scenes are in marked contrast with the body of the play
in structure and, in the opinion of many critics, in
versification as well. They must, nevertheless, have
been part of the original plan of the play, for the
death of Hector is foreshadowed in Andromache's
dream (V. iii). The repetition of the closing lines
of Act V, Scene iii, just before Pandarus' epilogue at
the end of the play, indicates some sort of revision
or change of plan. It may be that these closing scenes
are from an old play on which Shakespeare based his
work, or it may be simply that Shakespeare himself
lost interest in the play and supplied only a per-
functory ending. (See Appendix A.)

Troilus and Cressida has been so often used as evidence in attempts to interpret Shakespeare's spiritual
history through his plays that the question of the
authorship of this play leads not unnaturally to the
consideration of its value as a document for use in such
interpretation. This consideration involves the examination of the play not as an isolated literary phe-
nomenon but as a part of a large body of literature on
the subject of the Trojan war in which definite tradi-
tions and conceptions have become firmly established
and the outlines of character and incident sharply de-
fined. The play must, then, be regarded in its proper
setting, and the study of its meaning in relation to
Shakespeare's mind and experience cannot be divorced

from the consideration of its literary ancestry and the
tradition in which it belongs.

Troilus and Cressida makes an undeniably unpleasant impression upon the reader, particularly
when he views the play in the light of the modern
attitude toward the ancient heroes. The significance of
the play has long puzzled critics, so much so that its
interpretation has been called 'the chief problem in
Shakespeare.' The main answers proposed to the
question of the meaning of the play have been these:
that Shakespeare is here engaged in the famous War
of the Theatres, and in the characters of the play is
caricaturing his opponents in that controversy; that
Shakespeare's personal animosity against Chapman
is leading him to satirize Homer, whom Chapman was
translating; that Shakespeare is here writing a bitter
satire on Greek ideals; that he means to ridicule the
ideals of chivalry; and, finally, that the tone of the
play is the result of intense personal bitterness and disillusionment on the part of Shakespeare himself.

The theory that this play is a document in the War
of the Theatres springs from a remark in the Second
Part of the *Return from Parnassus*, a play acted at
Cambridge and written about January, 1602. In this
play Kempe declares that 'our fellow Shakespeare hath
given him (Jonson) a purge that made him beray his
credit.' It has been assumed that *Troilus and Cressida*
is that purge, but Dr. R. A. Small has shown that
there is no ground for identifying the characters in
the play with the participants in that controversy,
with the possible exception that the character of Ajax
may have been intended as a caricature of Jonson.[1]
Professor Tatlock shows that even this is impossible,[2]

[1] Small, R. A., *The Stage-Quarrel between Ben Jonson
and the so-called Poetasters*, Breslau, 1899, pp. 153-171.
[2] Tatlock, J. S. P., 'The Siege of Troy in Elizabethan
Literature, etc.,' *Pub. Mod. Lang. Assn.*, xxx, 726-734.

so that the theory that this play had to do with the quarrel between Jonson and the Poetasters is without adequate foundation.

The other explanations of the play become equally unsatisfactory when the literary pedigree of *Troilus and Cressida* is considered. Chaucer regarded the conduct of his Criseyde in the light of the curiously artificial ideals of courtly love. Long before Shakespeare's time these ideals had been forgotten, and the mediæval love-allegory survived only in form; its spirit was dead. In the fifteenth century the story of Criseyde was carried on from the point at which Chaucer left it, in *The Testament of Cresseid,* a poem by Robert Henryson, a Scottish schoolmaster. The standards by which Chaucer judged his heroine had already been forgotten, and to Henryson Criseyde was little better than a harlot. This poem was included in all the sixteenth century editions of Chaucer, and was generally believed to have been written by him in spite of the fact that Henryson refers to him more than once in the poem. Henryson entirely altered Chaucer's conception of the character of Criseyde, and his view became traditional. Long before Shakespeare's time Cressida's reputation as a loose woman had become firmly established and too familiar to admit of change. All through the sixteenth century a woman 'of Cressid's kind' was proverbially a harlot, and Shakespeare only followed the fashion which he could hardly have altered had he wished to. When her treatment at the hands of other writers of the sixteenth century is considered, it seems remarkable that Shakespeare dealt with her so gently, not that he was so severe with her.

The same thing is true of the attitude of Shakespeare's predecessors and contemporaries toward the characters of Troilus and Pandarus. Troilus was traditionally the fiery young lover, as he appears in this

play, and the outlines of the character of Pandarus
were definitely fixed in the popular imagination. In
fact his name had become the common noun, pander,
long before Shakespeare was born. The dramatist's
attitude toward the characters in the love story was
the only possible one in his day, and he merely took
the material as he found it, definitely crystallized in
form, and intensified it.

The parts of the play dealing with the Greek and
Trojan heroes must be considered in much the same
way. Homer was regarded by the Elizabethans with
none of the reverence which he excites in our own
day, and was generally known to them in bad translations, if at all. The story of the Greeks and the
Trojans was read chiefly in mediæval versions, and
mediæval tradition dealt severely with the ancient
heroes. This tradition created a feeling of hostility
toward the Greeks, largely because of the belief that
both English and Western Europeans generally were
of Trojan descent. The belief in a line of mythical
British sovereigns descended from Brutus, the great-
grandson of Æneas, persisted down to the time of
Milton.

The characters of Ajax and Thersites, which have
furnished the basis of most of the criticism of Shakespeare's treatment of the heroes must also be considered with reference to their literary pedigree. Ajax
as a comic figure is well established in earlier literature. The incident of his insanity and consequent
slaughter of the sheep seems to have particularly ap-
pealed to the Elizabethan imagination, which always
regarded insanity as funny, and the pun on 'Ajax' and
'a jakes' (see note on III. iii. 245, 246) had long been
popular. The character of Ajax in *Troilus and Cressida* is developed from the traits generally attributed
to him, and the conception of him as the arrogant
blockhead is largely the traditional one.

The scurrility of Thersites, which serves as a sort of foul chorus to the play, is unpleasant, but Thersites, as he appears in this play, is directly derived from the *Iliad*. His position in the play is that of the stock Fool, who appears again and again in the Elizabethan drama, and it is unlikely that an Elizabethan audience would have found him anything but amusing. The effects of *Troilus and Cressida* are those of vivid contrast and heightened color, not those of subtlety, and Thersites is the type of the vulgar railer as Cressida is that of the light-hearted coquette.

It is not true, moreover, that all the camp scenes in the play are unpleasant or all the warriors base. Hector, Ulysses, and Nestor are admirable figures in many ways, and the scenes in which they appear were plainly written with the author's keenest sympathy and interest. Their speeches are frequently rich in both wisdom and poetry, and they seem to be the creation of an artist working for his own satisfaction rather than that of a satirist of contemporary individuals or ancient literary conceptions.

There is little to say in defense of the theory that this play sprang from the personal bitterness and disillusionment of its author. The facts of his life, as far as we know them, give no ground for such a belief, and Shakespeare, moreover, was one of the most objective of dramatists. If this theory were to be accepted it would be necessary to disregard the literary history of the story of Troy and its main figures in order to give a subjective explanation of a play by a remarkably objective writer. Shakespeare seldom unlocked his heart in his plays, and, as his latest biographer remarks, 'we make of the drama a poor thing indeed if we do not allow a great literary artist to portray so well-known and conventionalized a story without accusing him of dragging before the public

his own more sordid experiences.'[1] The unpleasant
effect of the play may be largely attributed to two
things: the nature of the material which the author
used and the confusion and want of internal harmony
in the play as he left it. There is little evidence to
justify the supposition of a bitter spiritual crisis in
the poet's life as the explanation of its tone.[2]

Troilus and Cressida must, then, be studied in its
relation to the body of literature from which it sprang.
Its treatment of the young lovers and of the heroes of
antiquity can be completely understood only when we
throw off the conceptions which are universal in our
day but were unknown in Shakespeare's. It is essential to see the play as an Elizabethan would have seen
it, against the background of the early seventeenth
century, not against that of the twentieth. The most
recent and complete judgment of the play is ad-
mirably summed up by Professor Tatlock in these
words:

'Shakespeare came to the material of this play, then,
precisely as he came to that of the English historical
plays, finding incidents and characters largely fixed
beforehand, and too intractable to be greatly modified,
even had he wished to modify them. It is as a historical play, in the Elizabethan sense, that it should be
regarded; often serious, sometimes verging on the
tragic, but pervaded with comedy. It has been mis-
understood because our feeling toward the sources of

1 Adams, J. Q., *A Life of William Shakespeare,* Boston
and New York, 1923, p. 353.
2 Mrs. O. C. Campbell, in the *London Mercury* (vol. iv,
no. 19, pp. 48-59), justifies the play from the point of view
of the art of the drama rather than from that of historical
perspective. She feels that Shakespeare is here concerned
with the degrading effect of war, and especially with its
cruel futility and its destruction of many of the finer qualities in human nature. The number of performances of the
play since the beginning of the Great War may indicate
that it touched the human experience of the war years.

its story has changed. Those who approach it from
the classical side may find gloom and satire; those who
come, as its author did, from the medieval, will find
chivalry and humor.'[1]

[1] Tatlock, J. S. P., 'Troilus and Cressida,' in *The Tudor
Shakespeare,* New York, 1912, pp. xix, xx.

APPENDIX D

The text of the present edition is based, by permission of the Oxford University Press, upon that of the Oxford Shakespeare, edited by the late W. J. Craig, which has been collated with the Folio of 1623 and the Quarto of 1609. The following deviations have been made from Craig's text:

1. The stage-directions are those of the Folio, necessary additional words being inserted in square brackets.

2. Words or lines occurring in the Quarto and not in the Folio have been enclosed in square brackets.

3. Many changes in punctuation, not affecting the meaning of the passages involved, have been made without comment. The spelling has been normalized in a number of cases: e.g. relics (reliques), antics (anticks), mastic (mastick), cried (cry'd), blackamoor (black-a-moor), forgo (forego), warlike (war-like), godlike (god-like), to-morrow (to morrow), anything (any thing), everywhere (every where), everything (every thing), and Greek for Grecian in stage-directions and Dramatis Personæ. The spellings Troyan for Trojan, burthen for burden, and murtherer for murderer have been restored. Negociations, dependance, and dependant have been replaced by negotiations, dependence, and dependent, corpse by corse, and swounding by swooning.

4. The Folio has been followed in the use of such elisions as th' and i' th', and in the contractions of many endings.

5. The following alterations of the text have been made, the readings of the present edition preceding and those of Craig following the colon. Except in

two cases otherwise marked the changes represent a
return to the Folio text:

	The Prologue: Prologue
Prol. 17	Antenonidus: Antenorides
I. i. 5	hath: has
15	farther: further
16	must needs: must
33	then she comes, when she is thence.: 'when she comes'!—When is she thence?
ii. 1, 2, 12, 16, 34, 39, 41	*Man.: Alex.*
31	purblinded: purblind
90	will: wit
169	two-and-fifty: one-and-fifty
173	Two-and-fifty: One-and-fifty
205	judgment: judgments
250	helm: helmet
257	money: an eye
280	another: a
318	That: Then
	contents: content
iii. 8	diverts: divert
19	think: call
	shame?: shames?
27	loud: broad
67	the heavens ride,: heaven rides,
	Greeks': the Greekish
121, 123	an: a
127	is it: it is
128	in: with
168	as like: like
169	god: good
186	who,: whom,
190	and keeps: keeps
194	comparisons: comparison
202	call: calls
210	guide: guides
228	on: bid
256	loud,: aloud,
290	I'll be: I am
294	nobleman: noble man
333	Who: whom
334	his honour: those honours
336	this: the
352	from hence receives: receives from hence
368	wear: share

387	Now, Ulysses,: Ulysses, Now
II. i. 15	you: thou
31	in: of
67	I do so.: so I do.
69	whosomever: whosoever
108	E'en: Even
111	He: a'
117	war: wars
119, 120	To Achilles, to Ajax, to—: to, Achilles! to, Ajax! to!
140	'Tis: it is
ii. 52	What's: What is
71	sieve (Q): sink
97	what shriek is this?: what shriek?
104	old,: eld,
105	can: canst
106	clamour!: clamours!
147	pleasures: pleasure
185	nation: nations
iii. 81	emulations,: emulous
91	so say: say so
96	it is: 'tis
97	the: a
110	counsel that: composure
128	of: on
132	came: come
136	tends: tend
140	lines,: lunes,
163	it: pride
188	'gainst itself.: down himself:
191	greet: meet
242	doth: does
255	she: her
256	Fame: Fam'd
III. i. 34	who's: who is
48	measure: measures
89	very, very: very
96	*Helen.* You must not know where he sups.: You must know where he sups. (Continued to Pandarus.)
106 133, 135, 137,	instrument now,: instrument. Now,
138	Oh! ho!: O! O!
ii. 3	*Man.: Boy.*
20	palates taste: palate tastes
23	and: tun'd

128	but not, till now,: but, till now, not
141	My soul of counsel from me.: My very soul of counsel.
157, 158	Where is my wit? / I would be gone.: I would be gone. / Where is my wit?
159	speaks: speak
183	Wants: Want
198	they've: they have
199	as wind,: wind,
	as sandy: sandy
216	chamber whose bed (Dyce): chamber and a bed, which bed
iii. 4	love,: come,
11	am: have
43	bent, why turn'd, on him.: bent on him.
49	proud: poor
55	What comes: What! comes
81	honour'd: honour
82	place,: places,
86	Doth: Do
110	married: mirror'd
116	is: be
120	reverb'rate: reverberates
137	feasting: fasting
144	nor: or
168	The welcome: welcome
198	Pluto's: Plutus'
226	airy air: air
254	an: a
282	captain, general: captain-general
297	buy: be wi'
312	carry: bear
IV. i. 16	meets,: meet,
32	despiteful'st: despiteful
36	it was: 'twas
44	whereof.: wherefore:
66	which heavier: the heavier
ii. 10	eyes: joys
19	What, 's all: What! are all
35	i' th': o' the
69	concluded so?: so concluded?
83	Ah! ha!: Ah! ah!
112	I will: I'll
iv. 11	A sweet duck!: Ah! sweet ducks.
18	where: when
32	Is 't: Is it
48	Distasting: distasted

77	gift: gifts
79	novelties: novelty
82	afraid.: afear'd.
103	Whiles: While
132	know, my lord,: know you, lord,
138	we: you
142	in: to
v. 2	time. With: time with
2, 3	courage, Give: courage. Give
41	You are: You're
50	his—: his.
55	a language: language
103	impair: impure
175	Who: Whom
181	*Hect.: Hec.*
186	And seen thee scorning: Despising many
189	unto: to some
234	prithee;: pray thee:
251	the: an
271	you. Afterwards,: we afterwards,
280	on heaven nor on earth,: upon the heaven nor earth,
V. i. 21	guts-griping: the guts-griping,
27	tetter, and the like, take: tetter, take
73	Hoy-day!: Hey-day!
103	foretell it, that it: foretell it: it
109	after—nothing: after. Nothing
ii. 21	a forsworn—: forsworn
68	Give't me: Give't to me
84	It is: 'Tis
111	say,: said,
136	are: be
166	in: on
189	will: would
iii. 4	gone.: in:
82	doth: do
114-116	*Pan.* Why, but hear you! *Tro.* Hence, brother lackey! Ignomy and shame Pursue thy life and live aye with thy name!: omitted
iv. 9	of: on
10	tother: other
20	th'other: t'other
v. 11	Polyxenes: Polixenes
24	straying: strawy
vi. 13	do I: I do
	Have at: Ha! have at

17	befriends: befriend
26	thou: I
vii. 6	arms: aims
14, 16, 25	*Bast.: Mar.*
viii. 16	*Greek.: Myr.*
ix. 2	Sold[iers].: omitted
x. 35	mine: my
39	desir'd,: loved,
48	Pandar's: pander's

APPENDIX E

Suggestions for Collateral Reading

William Caxton: *The Recuyell of the Historyes of Troy,* edited by H. O. Sommer, London, 1894, 2 vols.

Geoffrey Chaucer: *The Book of Troilus and Criseyde,* edited by R. K. Root, Princeton, 1926.

John Lydgate: *Lydgate's Troy Book,* edited by H. Bergen for the Early English Text Society, London, 1906-1910, 3 vols.

Robert Henryson: *The Testament of Cresseid.* In *The Works of Geoffrey Chaucer,* edited by W. W. Skeat, Oxford, 1894-1897, Vol. VII. (*Chaucerian and Other Pieces.*)

Thomas Heywood: *The Iron Age.* In *The Dramatic Works of Thomas Heywood,* London, 1874, vol. 3.

John S. P. Tatlock: 'The Siege of Troy in Elizabethan Literature, especially in Shakespeare and Heywood,' *Publications of the Modern Language Association of America,* xxx (1915), 673-770. (The part of the article dealing primarily with Shakespeare begins at p. 726. This admirable article, upon which all recent criticism of the play largely depends, is indispensable to the student of the play.)

——'The Chief Problem in Shakespeare,' *Sewanee Review,* xxiv (1916), 129-147. (The conclusions reached in the article just referred to are here restated in somewhat more popular form.)

Roscoe A. Small: *The Stage-Quarrel between Ben Jonson and the So-called Poetasters,* Breslau, 1899, pp. 139-171.

Hyder E. Rollins: 'The Troilus-Cressida Story from Chaucer to Shakespeare,' *Publications of the Modern Language Association of America,* xxxii (1917), 383-429.

William W. Lawrence: 'The Love Story in *Troilus and Cressida.*' In *Studies by Members of the Department of English and Comparative Literature in Columbia University,* New York, 1916, pp. 187-211.

Joseph Q. Adams: *A Life of William Shakespeare,* Boston and New York, 1923, pp. 345-354.

——'*Timon of Athens* and the Irregularities in the First Folio,' *Journal of English and Germanic Philology,* vii (January, 1908), 53-63.

Agnes M. Mackenzie: *The Women in Shakespeare's Plays,* New York, 1924, pp. 183-200.

Olwen C. Campbell: '*Troilus and Cressida:* A Justification,' *London Mercury,* vol. iv, no. 19 (May, 1921), pp. 48-59.

The edition of the play by J. S. P. Tatlock in the *Tudor Shakespeare,* published in 1912, has a valuable introduction and the excellent text edited for the *Cambridge Shakespeare* by William Allen Neilson in 1906. The edition by K. Deighton for the *Arden Shakespeare,* published in 1906, has much interesting and useful material in its notes. William J. Rolfe's edition, published in 1882, also provides much valuable information. Most of the nineteenth century criticism of *Troilus and Cressida* has been rendered obsolete by more modern examination of the background of the play, especially by the articles of Professors Tatlock and Rollins above referred to.

INDEX OF WORDS GLOSSED

(Figures in full-faced type refer to page-numbers)

rode on his tide: **50** (II. iii. 142)

roisting: **45** (II. ii. 208)

rounded in: **25** (I. iii. 196)

roundly: **67** (III. ii. 161)

ruder: **62** (III. ii. 24)

rule, specialty of: **21** (I. iii. 78)

ruth: **120** (V. iii. 48)

ruthful: **120** (V. iii. 48)

salt: **32** (I. iii. 371)

sanctimony: **116** (V. ii. 136)

sans: **22** (I. iii. 94)

sarcenet: **107** (V. i. 36)

savage strangeness: **50** (II. iii. 136)

scaffoldage: **24** (I. iii. 156)

scants: **90** (IV. iv. 47)

scar: **7** (I. i. 116)

sculls: **125** (V. v. 22)

scurril: **24** (I. iii. 148)

seam: **52** (II. iii. 197)

secure: **38** (II. ii. 15)

see: **91** (IV. iv. 57)

seeming: **24** (I. iii. 157)

seethes: **57** (III. i. 44)

seizure: **5** (I. i. 59)

seld: **100** (IV. v. 149)

self-admission: **52** (II. iii. 178)

self-affected: **54** (II. iii. 253)

self-breath: **52** (II. iii. 184)

sennet: **18** (I. iii. S. d.)

sense (feeling): **33** (II. i. 23)

sense (perception): **73** (III. iii. 106)

sequest'ring: **69** (III. iii. 8)

serpigo: **48** (II. iii. 82)

set: **36** (II. i. 93)

severally: **104** (IV. v. 273)

'sfoot: **46** (II. iii. 6)

sharpens: **113** (V. ii. 72)

she: **18** (I. ii. 312)

shent: **48** (II. iii. 87)

shivers: **34** (II. i. 42)

short-armed: **46** (II. iii. 15)

show (external appearance): **20** (I. iii. 46)

show (reflect): **71** (III. iii. 48)

shrewdly gor'd: **77** (III. iii. 229)

sick: **23** (I. iii. 132)

sieve: **40** (II. ii. 71)

signify: **100** (IV. v. 154)

sinister: **99** (IV. v. 127)

Sir Valour: **25** (I. iii. 176)

sith: **19** (I. iii. 13)

sleave silk: **107** (V. i. 35)

sleeveless: **123** (V. iv. 9)

smart: **89** (IV. iv. 19)

so: **43** (II. ii. 145)

soil: **43** (II. ii. 148)

soilure: **83** (IV. i. 56)

Sol: **22** (I. iii. 89)

sole pure: **27** (I. iii. 244)

sooth: **58** (III. i. 60)

sort (lot): **32** (I. iii. 376)

sort (manner): **82** (IV. i. 23)

sorts: **7** (I. i. 111)

soul of counsel: **66** (III. ii. 141)

specialty of rule: **21** (I. iii. 78)

speculation: **73** (III. iii. 109)

sped: **61** (III. i. 157)

sperr up: **1** (Prol. 19)

spite: **126** (V. v. 41)

spleen (amusement): **25** (I. iii. 178)

spleen, weakest: **42** (II. ii. 128)

spleens, heaving: **45** (II. ii. 196)

sportful: **30** (I. iii. 335)

sprite: **63** (III. ii. 32)

spritely: **44** (II. ii. 190)

square: **115** (V. ii. 129)

stain: **8** (I. ii. 27)

stale: **53** (II. iii. 203)

stand the push: **43** (II. ii. 137)

starting: **94** (IV. v. 2)

starts: **114** (V. ii. 98)

state (council): **55** (II. iii. 274)

state (statecraft): **76** (III. iii. 203)

state (government): **104** (IV. v. 263)

stick: **68** (III. ii. 202)

still (silent): **25** (I. iii. 200)

still (ever): **102** (IV. v. 194)

stirring: **51** (II. iii. 147)

stithied: **104** (IV. v. 254)

stomach: **37** (II. i. 137)

straight: **62** (III. ii. 16)

strain: **73** (III. iii. 112)

strain, make no: **30** (I. iii. 326)

strait: **75** (III. iii. 154)

strange: **54** (II. iii. 253)

strangeness, savage: **50** (II. iii. 136)

stretch'd: **24** (I. iii. 156)

subscribe: **51** (II. iii. 157)

substance: **30** (I. iii. 324)

subtle: **116** (V. ii. 148)

success: **42** (II. ii. 117)

suffer: **85** (IV. ii. 30)

sufferance (endurance): **4** (I. i. 30)

sufferance (suffering and by permission): **36** (II. i. 104)

suffocate: **23** (I. iii. 125)

suited: **1** (Prol. 24)

sunburnt: **28** (I. iii. 282)

suppose: **19** (I. iii. 11)

surety (feeling of security): **38** (II. ii. 14)

surety (assurance): **112** (V. ii. 58)

sway: **20** (I. iii. 60)

swoln: **52** (II. iii. 185)

tables: **97** (IV. v. 60)

tabourines: **105** (IV. v. 274)

taint: **32** (I. iii. 374)

take 't off: **15** (I. ii. 221)

tame: **70** (III. iii. 10)

tapster's arithmetic: **11** (I. ii. 121)

tarre: **32** (I. iii. 391)

taste (foretaste): **70** (III. iii. 13)

taste (suggestion): **115** (V. ii. 124)

tasted: **65** (III. ii. 97)

tax: **25** (I. iii. 197)

tell a pin: **111** (V. ii. 21)

tempers: **20** (I. iii. 57)

tends: **50** (II. iii. 136)

testern: **ix** (Ep. 29)

tetchy: **6** (I. i. 101)

tetter: **106** (V. i. 27)

that (in that): **41** (II. ii. 93)

that (because): **60** (III. i. 131)

Thetis: **20** (I. iii. 39)

thicker: **63** (III. ii. 36)

thievery: **90** (IV. iv. 43)

through: **54** (II. iii. 236)

thwarted: **107** (V. i. 42)

tickling: **97** (IV. v. 61)

tide: **109** (V. i. 92)

tide, rode on his: **50** (II. iii. 142)

tisick: **122** (V. iii. 101)

Titan: **132** (V. x. 25)

tithe: **38** (II. ii. 19)

to (in addition to): **3** (I. i. 7)

to (with): **58** (III. i. 64)

to 't: **104** (IV. v. 261)

toast: **20** (I. iii. 45)

took: **70** (III. iii. 19)

topless deputation: **24** (I. iii. 152)

tortive: **19** (I. iii. 9)

touch (trait): **75** (III. iii. 175)

touch (feeling): **87** (IV. ii. 104)

touch'd: **40** (II. ii. 76)